'Take what you want', said God,
'and pay for it.'

Charge

ARTHUR SELDON

TEMPLE SMITH · LONDON

First published in Great Britain 1977
by Maurice Temple Smith Ltd
© Arthur Seldon 1977
ISBN 0 85117 115X cased
ISBN 0 85117 1303 paperback
Printed in Great Britain by
Billing & Sons Ltd
Guildford, London & Worcester

Contents

Tables

Acknowledgements

I am grateful to Charles Rowley, Professor of Economics at the University of Newcastle, for scrutinising the theoretical passages on the nature of public goods; to Ralph Harris, General Director of the Institute of Economic Affairs, for detailed comments and, more generally, for twenty years of stimulating partnership that has refined ιny thinking; to Stephen Haseler, of the City of London Polytechnic and the G.L.C., for criticisms on an early draft; to John Mills, Deputy Leader of Camden Council, for reading several chapters and pulling no Fabian punches; to Sudha Shenoy, a young leader in Britain of the revived Austrian School of Economics, for Whiggish suggestions on sharpening the argument; and to scores of IEA authors from whom I have learned much down the years. None would accept all I say; some would differ mildly, several sharply.

I am also indebted to Marjorie Seldon for judgement on how people might react to several proposals and for specific suggestions; and to Maurice Temple Smith for general advice, astringent opinion and discerning editing.

Not least, I should like to thank Michael Solly for acting as literary longstop; Ken Smith for prompt discovery of elusive references; and Joan Roffey for good humour in transcribing tired longhand into pleasing typescript.

I have written this book as a personal venture. My views are not necessarily shared by anyone associated with the IEA.

For every man,
and perhaps even more for every woman,
unrepresented by political 'representatives',
to help them see
how they can run their lives,
themselves,
at last.

PART 1

Populism and Prices

1 Pundits, politicians and people

Our world has largely been shaped by the thinking of scholars, academics, experts, specialists, writers, teachers – the 'pundits'. For years, decades, centuries, they have debated among themselves and influenced the actions and policies of leaders and statesmen.

This direct influence of paternalist ideas on action was inevitable and possibly desirable up to about a century ago when ordinary people lacked the knowledge or the resources to participate in the formation of policy. But the pundits have continued to talk to one another, mostly far over the heads of the people, for a century in which there has been increasing education and enlightenment, understanding and responsibility. Under their advice the politicians have created institutions and services – from schools, transport, and hospitals to libraries, nurseries and abbatoirs – for the good (they said) of the people. They have also created electoral machinery – 'representative democracy' – to enable the people to show their approval or disapproval.

But something has gone wrong. The machinery – Parliament, the ballot box, representative democracy – has never worked effectively. The machinery of representation does not represent individual members of the public but the organised groups that claim to speak for them. As a result the institutions have increasingly diverged from the wishes or preferences of the people as individuals. Some of them – such as law and defence – were necessary and desirable when they were created down the centuries, and in principle remain so. Others – many or most of the nationalised industries, welfare services and local government amenities – should never have been created, but are still seen as necessary, or as sanctified by time, long after the conditions that once seemed to justify them have passed into history.

The central position from which this book starts is this: how can we decide what services the government ought to provide, and how can we make them fit more closely the needs and wishes of the ordinary people for whom they are supposed to be provided?

At present, the only or main control on government services is political, through the institutions of representative democracy. This device is necessary (though faulty) for the institutions and services that *only* government can provide: but it is far too crude for all the personal services, from medical care and housing to car-parking, that could be provided in response to individual preferences. It is crude because the ballot box does not record and is not geared for supplying individual requirements. Despite that decisive disqualification, government is still unnecessarily used for a vast range of institutions supplying personal services that individuals could provide themselves.

Resistance to reform

What services should government provide? How should we pay for them? How much of what government now provides could and should be provided outside government?

The only way to discover the answers to these questions is to establish machinery to record individual preferences and test new mechanisms outside government. We could then see which services do not have to be provided by government. But the pundits still largely advise, and the politicians still endlessly create, government institutions 'for the good of the people'. Their reputable reasons are that they continue to think that *all* the institutions they happen to have created in the last century are in principle still for the good of the people, or that they see no other way of adapting them to individual preferences except by variations within the existing arrangements (because 'we must start from here'). The less reputable – though understandable – reason is self-interested resistance to change by government employees whose jobs would be at risk. Too much time is therefore spent patching up government services (for which the public is forced to pay) instead of questioning their justification or very existence, and far too little on making room for new services for which the public would pay voluntarily. The cosy corner of politicians, bureaucrats and pundits resists change.

Even so, new ideas are coming to the fore as old ones are refined or discarded, and it is possible to see some politicians adopting new thinking as the changing abilities and attitudes of individual citizens make new institutions more timely or urgent – and therefore electorally more rewarding. But the resistance to reform from intellectual conviction and self-interest slows down adaptation to new conditions. It may be that the general public will have to participate more directly in the debate without the mediation (or barrier) of 'representatives'. To do so, it will need to understand what is at stake and indicate its readiness for change, or, better still, its anxiety for early reform. It does not have to burden itself with detail; but it must know the general principles.

The people must lead their leaders

This book is an effort to clarify for the general reader the debate between the pundits. It rests on a core of economic thinking that economists have been evolving and developing for two centuries – the notion of 'public goods'. They are still refining the idea and they draw different conclusions for policy from it. My interpretation of it is that the central truth is simple enough and its implication for policy clear enough for people in all schools of democratic political sympathy to accept and apply in practice. Moreover, I believe it resolves a difference of outlook that has deeply but unnecessarily divided the British people.

Public support for reform may have to assert itself all the more strongly in a representative democracy, where government yields to pressure from organised interests that stand to lose from change. Not only is there no machinery in representative democracy for asserting individual preferences over much of the services of contemporary government; the sizeable number of government employees who provide them invariably prevail over the much larger number who use and pay for them. It may be that the providers of government services are too powerful to be made subject to the sovereignty of the mass of consumers. In that event the outcome will be either a period of possibly benign paternalism or acquiescent conformity (such as in Sweden, at least until 1976) or a refusal to accept bureaucratic encroachment on personal and family lives. The resistance to taxation by avoidance (legal), evasion (illegal), power bloc organisation (the self-employed) and emigration do not indicate that the process of encroachment can continue much longer without provoking the very tension and social divisiveness that government services are supposed to prevent.

It may be that some of our leaders think further (or even existing) encroachment is generally desired. I do not recognise this as the preference of ordinary people. That is why I address this book to them. They could have much more say, informed by more knowledge of the world created for them. Politicians and pundits are welcome as eavesdroppers; some of them may see that there is a good case for creating effective machinery to record private preferences where 'representative' democracy is ineffective. In that sense the argument is not about philosophical value-judgements of ultimate right and wrong, but about the task of devising tools for the people to use themselves. This task has been largely neglected by all three British political parties for a century.

The unnecessary divide

This book questions conventional beliefs over a wide range of human activity, public and private. Some readers will find it startling, others common sense. But as it follows questioning and criticism with constructive proposals for reform, readers who persevere with the argument to the end will judge it better.

The central argument is derived from the main principles of economics, which are not difficult to grasp and which, once understood, make simple and clear what once seemed complex and difficult. Many of the basic truths of economics are refined common sense, though some may strike newcomers as surprising.

The book is written for three classes of readers. First, I intend it for everyone, in every walk of life, interested in himself, his causes and his country. It has a bearing on the way we run the family and the household as well as industry and government. Its second market is the general reader who wonders what economists are saying that can shed light on the issues of the day. The third market is the newcomer to economics at school or university who wants an unconventional entrée into the heart of economic thinking to accompany formal textbooks.

In the first market I shall be writing perhaps even more for women than for men. They are rather more numerous; but also they may respond more sensitively to the central theme than men. They are often less sentimental and more experienced in ensuring daily 'micro-economic' value for their money in shopping for themselves and for their families. They may see the good sense of what I shall be saying sooner than more politically-minded men whose seduction by (wrong) ideas and ideals in 'macro-economic' national affairs has, I would say, made possible the massive errors in public policy (and social policy in particular) of the last century, especially in the thirty years since World War II. It is man in the mass who can be most easily misled into applauding policies he would ridicule at home with his wife and family: and that is as true of xenophobic Conservatives as of class-obsessed trade unionists. Macro-man at mass factory meetings, mass marches or mass General Elections is seldom a good advertisement for humanity. Macro-woman has her moments. Both are better in micro-quantities.

Readers who want to know what economists are saying and debating will find the central issues discussed without jargon, or at least with the few necessary technical words explained in plain English. The man and woman who finishes this book will, I think, make more sense of — and take with a larger pinch of salt — 'what the papers say' as well as 'what the politicians preach'. It will help them understand the great debates of our day — how much income should be left to individuals to spend as they wish and how much should be taken by the state and spent for them; how much production must be left to or controlled by the state; how people can best pay for it; how much influence they can exert over it; how much choice families and households can exercise over their lives; how far our lives must be run by officials and politicians; and ultimately what bearing all this has on the choices between capitalism and communism or between social democracy and liberalism.

Students of economics will find the central principles applied to the real world in which they live and in which the issues and policies of the day will continue to be debated.

The reader does not require formal training to understand the essence of economics. Many non-economists grasp it intuitively better than some graduates in economics.

But you must be ready for some very unconventional and unfashionable thinking, and even more for unorthodox and provocative conclusions for public policy. This thinking will be quite different from what you have come to expect in the last ten years from every political party, from Conservative to Communist, and from every newspaper, from *The Times* to the *Morning Star*. But it is thinking that will have to be recognised and absorbed in the next twenty or thirty years if the liberal character and temper of British society is to be preserved. In this time the parties may have regrouped themselves and the newspapers may be replaced by other kinds of publication that belatedly reflect the thinking they have ignored for decades.

The conclusions for policy will apply to the whole range of human action, from the privacy of the family to the more public activity of government. I shall argue that almost every institution is run less effectively than it could be, with adverse effects on living standards and personal freedom, because it ignores a device that has been condemned in error by almost every school of thought for a century. Often the motives have been of the best; though they have also disguised other objectives far less worthy. At their best the inspiration has been the paternalist notion that people in authority, with a wider and longer view than the individual, could make better use of resources. At their worst, and more often, the impetus has been the authoritarian urge to win and exercise power in public life over other people who are thought incapable of choosing for themselves – or even of *learning* to choose, which is to take an even more scornful view of them. This paternalism suffuses British society. Pundits in politics, academia, the press and the pulpit *know* how the citizen should live, and they fight among themselves for the power to compel him, directly in politics or indirectly through influence on politicians.

These people have used plausible excuses for giving government more and more power to run society and provide people with their requirements. Their arguments have been mainly five. *Poverty*: some people, they said, could not provide essentials for themselves and their families out of their own means ('primary poverty'). *Irresponsibility*: the associated argument was that some people with enough means would be too foolish, short-sighted or callous to provide essentials for themselves or their families ('secondary poverty'). *Economy*: it was more efficient for government to provide basic essentials on a large scale for many people and without duplication. *Social (or 'external') benefits*: individuals or families would not engage at all, or sufficiently, in activities that benefited third parties, so government had to tax the people to provide the services, or provide them on a larger scale than individuals left to themselves. *Monopoly*: some essentials were most economically produced on such a large scale that only a small number of producers (perhaps only one) was likely, and that would give them power to exploit their fellows. These arguments, or pretexts, are examined later, together with a more recent sixth applying to the so-called basic national services: that government control and financing was desirable or necessary for management of the economy.

Public and private goods

All schools of thought have long agreed that some goods and services have to be provided by government. But in Britain and other Western countries government does far more. In Britain, it directly *produces* with its own employees about a third of the entire national output of goods and services. It *controls* or *influences* far more. It takes a further fifth of national income from individuals and firms and is supposed to redistribute it in cash, although, as we shall see, in large part it goes back to the same individuals. And it regulates and restricts much of the two-thirds of production run by private individuals and firms in order to ensure safety and other standards, or for more obscure or questionable reasons.

The third of the output of goods and services produced directly by government (national, regional or local) covers a wide range, from nuclear defence through police to adult evening classes in basket weaving. Some of them are what economists call public goods that must be produced collectively, by government, or not at all. The remainder could be produced by individuals or firms and offered on the market, so that consumers could choose between competing suppliers. The distinction between public and other goods is central to the argument of this book because public goods must be paid for by taxes and other goods can be paid for by charges.

Public goods have characteristics that distinguish them from other goods. They are necessarily provided for large groups of people in their catchment area. They are thus supplied jointly or collectively rather than separately to individuals or small groups. They require general agreement (ideally unanimous, but in the real, imperfect world only majority, or even minority) to pay jointly, that is, they require voluntary collective arrangements to coerce one another and also individuals who do not want the services at all but who cannot help benefiting from them. They are non-rival in the sense that, if they are used by more individuals, they can still be used by others – until a stage of full capacity and over-crowding; in other words, additional consumers can be serviced with no additional cost. Public goods thus render external benefits to third parties in the area who are not parties to the agreement. But the essential characteristic of public goods is that they cannot be refused to people who refuse to pay, and who would otherwise have a 'free ride' if they were not required to pay.

TABLE A: GOVERNMENT BY THE PEOPLE?
Or by unrepresentative minorities
since the second world war

General Election	Electorate (million)	CONSERVATIVE*				LABOUR				LIBERAL		
		Votes Cast (million)	Votes Won (million)	% of Votes Cast	% of Elec-torate	Votes Won (million)	% of Votes Cast	% of Elec-torate	Votes Won (million)	% of Votes Cast	% of Elec-torate
1945	32.84	24.98	9.96	39.87	30.33	11.99	48.00	36.50	2.25	9.00	6.85
1950	34.27	28.77	12.50	43.45	36.48	13.30	46.23	38.81	2.62	9.11	7.65
1951	34.63	28.60	13.72	47.97	39.61	13.95	48.78	40.28	0.73	2.55	2.11
1955	34.86	26.76	13.31	49.74	38.18	12.41	46.38	35.60	0.72	2.69	2.07
1959	35.40	27.86	13.75	49.35	38.84	12.22	43.86	34.52	1.64	5.88	4.64
1964	35.90	27.66	11.98	43.31	33.37	12.21	44.14	34.01	3.10	11.21	8.63
1966	35.96	27.26	11.42	41.89	31.76	13.06	47.91	36.32	2.33	8.55	6.48
1970	39.34	28.34	13.15	46.40	33.43	12.18	42.24	30.96	2.12	7.48	5.39
1974 (Feb)	39.75	31.33	11.96	38.17	30.09	11.65	37.18	29.31	6.06	19.34	15.26
1974 (Oct)	40.08	29.19	10.46	35.83	26.09	11.47	39.29	28.62	5.35	18.33	13.35

*Including Conservative allies

Public goods, to be produced at all, cannot therefore be produced in response to individual specification in the market: they must be financed collectively by the method known as taxation. Their benefits are provided to all the individuals in the catchment area, but the benefits cannot be paid for separately by individuals because they are inseparable, indivisible and indiscriminate.

All goods have some public qualities (a private house across the road may please you by its architecture or offend you by the colour of its front door). And all public goods yield private benefits (there is no more personal benefit than having your life saved by the armed forces). So there are no 'pure' or entirely public or private goods.

Most goods can be made by individuals or firms for other individuals or firms who will pay for them directly (food, clothing, books, homes, motor-cars and personal services of all types). But if people who refuse to pay for a commodity or service cannot be excluded, so that they have a 'free ride', no private person or company would produce it even though all or most individuals want it produced. This, then, is the characteristic that requires goods to be produced collectively by government for the people as a whole. All other goods are in this sense not 'public' and do not have to be produced collectively or paid for by taxes.

The archetypal public good is defence – national against external enemies and local against internal. Law itself is a public good from which all benefit jointly – or a public bad from which all suffer. Protection against contagious disease is another public good. A not obvious but important one is the production of knowledge and information. In these and other goods and services it is impossible to keep out people who will not pay. Anti-aircraft guns defend all people and property in the city against bombing. Police patrols or anti-malarial treatment of water protect everyone in the area.

Then there are goods and services from which people who refused to contribute could be excluded, but only at a cost that would make exclusion not worth the candle. Putting a high fence round a national park and posting ticket collectors on all the roads and paths entering it might cost more than would be raised in entrance fees.

I must add at once that, although government is the only method of producing public goods, it is a very imperfect solution, because it has no mechanism for measuring individual preferences in the kind and scale of public goods that people want. Government can use only the crude instrument of general elections every few years in which people are asked to vote for two or three parties each advocating 34, 57 or 86 varieties of policies. The party elected may – probably does – spend too much or too little on some services it provides, but voters cannot indicate their approval or disapproval of expenditure on, say, defence, overseas aid, commercial attaches, ante-natal clinics, or allotments.

Not least, although people must agree collectively to tax themselves to pay for public goods, they will not all put the value on them that is represented by their taxes. A person who opposes fluoridation must nevertheless pay for it in his rates or taxes if a majority agree it should be provided; and it is virtually impossible to go further and compensate people who object to public goods or who suffer from them (like those who are kept awake by street lighting).

Despite these objections, public goods must be produced by government or not at all, because some people will refuse to pay unless they are coerced by representative political democracy. If government confined itself to what are in this sense public goods it would be accepted as necessary. But does it? Are all the 'public' services, as they are beguilingly called, really public goods at all?

Keynes and the classics on public goods

The proper province of government has been a central concern of economists for two hundred years or more. Adam Smith, the founder of economics as a science, laid down the general principle that, apart from external defence and internal law and order, the state must also provide services that

> can never be for the interest of any individual, or small number of individuals, to erect and maintain: because the profit can never repay the expense to any individual or small number of individuals though it may frequently do much more than repay it to a great society.[111] *

Under this heading the Classical Economists who followed Adam Smith developed a list of state functions: some kinds of money, tax

* Superior numbers refer to books, etc. as sources, supporting argument or evidence, or that go into the subject further: References at end of book (p. 215).

collection, some education, welfare services, relief of some kinds of poverty, roads, bridges, canals, harbours.

Over twenty years ago[92] Lord Robbins, perhaps the most influential British liberal economist of our day, showed that J. M. Keynes, who was supposed to have destroyed classical economics and who still, thirty years after his death, dominates thinking in government, some British universities and the press, said much the same as Adam Smith. Keynes's formulation in a celebrated tract, *The End of Laissez Faire*, ran

> The most important Agenda of the state relate not to those activities which private individuals are already fulfilling but to those functions which fall outside the sphere of the individual, to those decisions which are made by no one if the state does not make them. The important thing for government is not to do things which individuals are doing already and to do them a little better or a little worse: but to do those things which are not done at all.[53]

Keynes's formulation is quite clear. The state should provide only those functions or services that individuals *could not* provide for themselves, that is public goods that cannot be refused to free riders who refuse to pay. Since Keynes is still usually claimed as a destroyer of classical economic philosophy in his best-known (1936) book, *The General Theory of Employment, Interest and Money*,[54] I should recall that Keynes reprimanded some of his followers as 'sour and silly' shortly before he died in 1946,[55] that no-one knows what he would be saying in 1977, that some economists argue his post-war followers, or at least some who claim his name as 'Keynesians', have misrepresented him, and his writings only a few years after *The General Theory* in 1938–9 suggest his name has been misappropriated. The Keynesians have usually ignored Keynes' declaration that he was not replacing but perfecting the classical system of thought and policy.

In his newest book,[94] the latest in a succession of works that should delight readers with their classical prose as well as their classical liberalism, Lord Robbins added a further guide to the scope for state action. It is 'to govern well, govern little', attributed to the eighteenth-century Marquis d'Argenson, a predecessor of early French economists whose crude thinking Adam Smith refined in his classic *The Wealth of Nations*. This warning to governments to keep off the people's grass, said Robbins, would have been respected by the

British classical economists for two reasons, both very central to this book. First, the government that developed under two centuries of state control, called the mercantile system, was inefficient and corrupt, as all government sooner or later tends to become. Second, the controls wielded by eighteenth-century government in England were harmful or superfluous; they either made no difference or, if they did, it was for the worse. And although the classical economists made a reasoned and subtle case for the state to provide defence and other services, *the case was not that the state would provide them satisfactorily but that no one else would provide them at all.* The classical formula was thus the same as Keynes': public goods. In short, the state was tolerated not as a desirable or efficient instrument, which a hundred years of Fabian and conservative paternalism has taught generations of teachers, but as *a necessary evil.* That is, efficient or not, corrupt or not, government *has* to produce public goods that individuals want but could not produce individually for one another. The notion of public goods thus provides a necessary but 'second best' justification for the state.

So far so clear. The classics and the moderns agree that some functions should be performed by the state because there is no other way. And we shall see later that state activity also has defects of its own – a concentration of power, high taxation, rationing by bureaucracy to replace the guideline of price – that must be weighed in the balance against the state doing anything unless its advantages over private action clearly and substantially exceed these defects. We shall also see that the advocates of government provision surprisingly overlook these incidental disadvantages of government activity.

Professor F. A. Hayek has lately questioned one of the functions of government that economists have accepted for two hundred years, that of providing money. He argues[37] that government has never provided a reliable, stable money: government-controlled money has stimulated inflation, economic instability (boom and slump), 'public' expenditure and economic nationalism. It was least harmful when controlled by the gold standard, but the best solution is to take money out of government hands and have it provided by competing private suppliers whose self-interest it would be to limit the supply in order to maintain the value.

A creaking hinge

The public goods formula for state action is thus a creaking hinge. It seems to be clear, at least as a principle, that, where individuals cannot be made to pay directly for a service they want, they must be compelled to pay by taxation or not have it provided at all. But it does not follow that government in practice will perform its function so as to achieve that purpose satisfactorily because it has severe defects of its own. And since people cannot indicate their opinion by making or withholding individual payment, we cannot even know whether people really want the public goods they are supposed to vote for by electing a party into office, or whether they want them to continue or discontinue once created.

Moreover, most of the 'government' sector in present-day Britain consists of goods and services that are not 'public goods'. They are produced by government, or so it is claimed, for the five main reasons I have described as 'plausible', by which I mean superficially persuasive but not really decisive. In other words, *most present-day British 'public' services do not have to be produced by government.* They could be produced by individuals, firms, voluntary organisations, cooperatives and other variants of *private* activity, catering directly to individual preferences.

Even those who believe that government should go on supplying these things still face a further and crucial question: is it best to continue financing them by taxes, the *collective* method, or by a method which links *individual* payment to *individual* benefit? This is the ground over which the battle rages. This book offers a solution that could commend itself to people who think themselves wide apart or even in opposite camps.

2 Price: barrier or missing link?

The great debate that has torn the British in two for a century has been over what is, at bottom, a simple error in reasoning. It lies at the root of unnecessarily big government, unnecessarily high taxation, avoidably large bureaucracies, and of their converse – unnecessarily restricted liberties, narrowed choices, discouragements to work and save.

The most common error lies deep in British social history and political thinking. It is buried in this familiar argument:

1 all people should have the minimum essentials for civilised living;
2 incomes are sometimes too low to pay for them;
3 therefore they should be provided free by the state.

This is the reasoning that has produced the apparently compassionate cry that a civilised society should not allow price to come between people and the essentials of life. Price was a 'barrier' to be destroyed. Lord Beveridge, in his famous 1942 report that inspired the post-war Labour-Liberal-Conservative welfare state, condemned it as an 'economic' barrier. The late Professor R. M. Titmuss, who influenced governmental and academic thinking on welfare policy in the 1950s and 1960s, inveighed against it as a 'price' barrier. A Minister of Health in the late 1960s, Mr Kenneth Robinson, later Chairman of the London Transport Executive, denounced it as a 'financial' barrier.

It is a misunderstanding of the function of price to think of it as a barrier between a would-be buyer and a service. Price is a neutral symptom of the deep-lying conditions in which we live: an imperfect world in which we have insufficient resources for everything we should like to do. We must therefore allocate those resources among numerous alternative uses. In this task we require a sign, or measure, or signal that tells us where resources are best used. We can then shift them from where they are used less well to where they are used better. Despite all the heat worked up about it as a 'barrier', price is *a tool that mankind cannot do without*. Before we go any further we must understand it and its qualities.

Price is neutral

Price is the sign, or measure, or signal that emerges spontaneously if people who want services talk terms to people who can supply them. Both groups can benefit by exchanging goods or services in a 'market' where people who want them are in contact with people who can supply them. In modern communities we exchange services for money, but money is only a convenient intermediary which simplifies agreement on prices. Ultimately we all exchange services: we give our services as butchers, bakers, builders, miners, railwaymen, engineers, teachers or doctors to others who give us their services as grocers, tailors, actors, writers, publishers, hoteliers or pilots. And price describes the terms on which we exchange, swap, trade, buy, sell and borrow – or, in short, serve one another. It is unique information created only by people coming together to exchange in the light of their unique knowledge of their affairs. The structure of prices is called the price 'system' and the whole social structure is called a market economy.

Price is useful

Price is not merely the fulcrum around which the market system turns. It is also the method of indicating the relative importance or 'value' of resources in alternative uses and the method of allocating resources to the best uses. People will pay more for something they value more than something else. This is not a perfect measure of the value of putting resources to different uses, but other methods are even more imperfect. In the popular catch-phrase, the price system is the worst in the world except all the others.

Price is pacific

In allocating labour, equipment, buildings, land and so on to the best uses, pricing automatically excludes other uses. Where this excluding function is not performed by market prices, and people differ about how to decide which uses are the best and which shall be excluded, they argue and debate and, in political democracies, organise political parties to gain power and compel minorities (or even majorities) to accept their way of deciding. They also, in Fascist and Communist societies, fight and kill one another. Pricing is a peaceful way of resolving argument and conflict.

This is true of families as well as nations. In the family, friction between a high-taxed father and growing children over the unrestrained use of the 'free' telephone, hot water, light, heat, or petrol is removed if they pay for it (out of earnings or even pocket money), because every single act of paying reminds them of the sacrifices they are making and induces them to think twice. Without pricing, the hard-pressed father has to go on reminding his forgetful offspring, and becomes stricter and less popular if they persistently ignore his reminders. With pricing the reminders appear spontaneously, without the personal appearance of an admonishing father. Pricing obviates instructions, commands, compulsion, sanctions, friction, disaffection, estrangement. Father does not have to demand 'cuts' in the use of services; the offspring make the 'cuts' in the light of knowledge of the cost to them of over-use.

Replace 'father' by 'government' and 'offspring' by 'consumers': the parallel is essentially complete. Churchill's 'Jaw, jaw; not war, war' is more likely if individuals in different countries haggle over prices than if their governments negotiate international deals or spheres of influence in which their peoples may trade, or raise barriers, enforced by law and arms, against trade.

Price is knowledge

Without price there is no guide to relative costs or values or the sacrifices required to obtain desired goods or services. Prices are imperfect guides because of monopoly, inequality in resources or information, and for other reasons; but without them buyers and sellers are blind. The absence of price in public goods, where price is impracticable, requires them to be controlled by government, that is, individual politicians and officials who must decide when to extend or contract them, or more fundamentally when to continue or discontinue them. But, in the absence of price, government must use even more crude indicators of the value of resources in different uses. In public goods government control is an unavoidable second best to pricing.

Price is non-authoritarian

If prices are not allowed to emerge spontaneously, the alternative is to apportion and allocate resources by authority vested in the state and working through officials. This, essentially, is the method used in the 'directed' or non-market economies in Eastern Europe and China and in some other countries in Asia and Africa. It is also the method used in Western democracies in services where the price 'barrier' is abolished, as in the British National Health Service, and state education and local government services supplied 'free' with no price charged to each 'customer'. *The alternative to allocation by price is thus allocation ('rationing') by government.* We must choose between the two. We cannot avoid rationing by pretending we have abolished price by supplying goods and services 'free'.

Price is a teacher

By creating and imparting information, price teaches care in comparing values, caution in making purchases, forethought in using services and resources, and husbandry and economy in managing money and household, business and national budgeting. Contrast the thoughtless use made of unpriced services (telephone, heating, the firm's stationery or the NHS) with the thoughtful shopping in the supermarket.

There is no third choice in the world as it is other than rationing by price or by direction. The way out for the people who like neither is to escape from reality by imagining that humans are selfless or resources infinite, so that rationing is unnecessary. There can be many individual or group acts of selfless giving in a free society, but we are not living in a world where everyone will give enough to everyone else, where most people will permanently make an effort without reward. Until that day comes, the Utopians are not helping the poor by their dreams.

If politicians were always benevolent and officials all-wise and fully informed about people's wishes, they could conceivably arrive at better terms for exchange and better rationing of resources than would be produced by prices arising from spontaneous exchange between individuals (or families, households, voluntary groups and associations, partnerships, firms, companies). But politicians have their own objectives to pursue – power, prestige, wealth, ideology – and once they obtain power they do not let it go easily. In directed economies the parties not in power, even where not suppressed, do not have much of a chance to replace the party that is in power. Even in market economies where government, as in Britain, controls a large part of activity, the parties have become skilled at staying in power by altering the general tempo of economic activity between General Elections and engineering changes in employment and inflation so that they win electoral praise for high employment and avoid blame for high inflation.

Still more importantly, officials cannot possibly know all the information that is in the heads or records of millions of people about which services they want and which they can supply. Some economists have argued that prices can be used in societies where the government owns and controls resources and that computers would enable the central authority to set prices and make decisions on the allocation of resources more efficiently than a market system.[56] To some extent pricing is used in Hungary, Yugoslavia and other communist countries. But by the time all the prices are collected by the central authority and the orders to switch resources have been transmitted and put into effect by the hundreds of thousands of managers of factories, offices, dockyards, mines, railways, universities, schools, warehouses and so on, the wants of the millions of individuals and techniques of production have changed. In such a system the use of resources in practice lags behind people's wishes and preferences. Even worse, authority is tempted to modify these preferences, reinterpret them in a way that suits itself, or ignore them. In time, perhaps, people may protest; but, short of civil war, their power to see that their preferences are respected is much weaker than in a market system where suppliers of services who do not satisfy them can be abandoned for others who do.

In a market system the control over the use of resources, and over those who own or manage them, arises from *choice* between *competing* suppliers. Where choice and competition are impracticable or uneconomic (that is, in public goods) other controls are required. Even then the problems and tensions of rationing remain in the political market, where they may take more violent means to resolve. Economists distinguish the private market, where goods and services are produced, allocated and exchanged by personal decisions guided by price, from the political market, in which people decide collectively the production and allocation of public goods, and the charity market, in which individuals separately or collectively allocate gifts. The private market has been studied intensively for two hundred years or more, the political market with the same intensity only for some twenty years, and the charity market only for some ten years. [50, 81, 114]

Price is unavoidable

Price is (except in public goods) ultimately unavoidable. It is like a plant that grows through all the obstacles in its way. It cannot be suppressed by law because it is a symptom of the urge of people, everywhere, to come together as buyers and sellers. Even if the state could inspect every human activity and every home, prices would emerge. In directed economies, in wartime Fascist Germany and peacetime Communist countries, something of the sort was and is attempted: officials are employed, or people enthusiastic for the regime are encouraged, to watch for and report outbreaks of unofficial pricing. Even in countries such as Britain attempts are sometimes made (espcially in war but also in peace, as in the Price Code and incomes policies) to suppress unofficial free pricing. And again people are encouraged to watch out for 'offenders'. Yet the most rigidly directed economies find it expedient to turn a blind eye to spontaneous pricing when, as periodically in Russia, authority thinks its official centralised allocations have gone too far and are discouraging production by weakening the urge of people to serve one another as buyers and sellers. If they are forbidden by the state and its 'law', they come together in 'black' (or 'grey') markets, which save the system from seizure by economic arthritis. In Russia, although it claims to be a centrally planned state with no individuals making money out of private activity, there is spontaneous pricing in agriculture, housebuilding, medical services and other activities difficult to control from the centre.[68] In Britain, and other countries in Europe, the suppression of spontaneous pricing of labour in 'incomes policies' is, after a year or so, increasingly evaded by reclassifying an employee to justify a higher rate of pay, by premature promotion, by creating other forms of payment like fringe benefits, and so on. And in the government services, pricing breaks out in bribes and corruption. It cannot be prevented merely by passing laws against it. Pricing is mightier than government.

So pricing is neutral, useful, pacific, informative, a teacher, non-authoritarian and irrepressible. Politicians, sociologists and others who denounce it as a barrier are therefore uncomprehending and futile. It should be understood and welcomed as an indicator of relative wants and relative scarcities. It conveys *knowledge* that makes the use of resources better informed and therefore more efficient; and, whatever methods are evolved in non-market, directed economies, they are all essential to replace the *information* that a price system supplies. To denounce price as a barrier is to blame it for reflecting the underlying scarcity of resources.

The missing link

We can go further than that. A price is better thought of not as a barrier but as its opposite – a *link* between buyer and seller. If it is irrepressible, it is better brought out into the open and made as serviceable an instrument as it can be in achieving the best use of resources. And this means refining it, rather than trying to suppress it: *making as much rather than as little use of it as possible* to yield information on relative valuations and costs, so that we are aware of the alternatives we forego in using resources for, say, hospitals rather than housing, swimming pools rather than police, Concordes rather than motor cars. The central theme of this book, indeed, is that the absence of prices as landmarks, benchmarks, bearings and signposts causes confusion, distortion and waste, and their restoration wherever possible is essential in making the best use of resources, whatever their use – consumption, investment, charity or anything else

This conclusion is clearly illustrated from three elemental services whose prices we in Britain have been increasingly trying to suppress: education since 1870, housing since 1915, medical care since 1948. How to use price as much as possible in all three is discussed in Chapters 4, 5 and 6, and in other services in Chapters 7, 8 and 9.

The mighty 'margin'

Economic reasoning can shed light on how pricing helps in making decisions that affect vast resources.

In the real world – whether in government, industry or the family, in spending, saving or indeed giving – the decision is not between the *whole* of one product or service and another. A government has to decide between a *little* more expenditure on, say, hospitals at the expense of a decrease in expenditure on, say, housing, or between higher farming subsidies (to save rural seats) and lower commuter fares (to win suburban seats). A local authority has to choose between spending more on swimming pools at the expense of more on police. A family that wants to spend more on its home has to spend less on holidays. Anyone who wants to spend more altogether has to save less (or borrow more). A charity or a philanthropist who wants to give more to an old people's home has less to give to an orphanage. Choices at the margin have to be made in all three markets – private, political, charity. There is no escape in wishful thinking, denouncing wicked capitalists, indulging compassion, or assuming that scarcity has been replaced by superabundance.

These increases and decreases are the 'margins' that economists analyse in the 'law of diminishing marginal utility', which explains how expenditure is apportioned among all the uses to which it can be put. The economic law that emerges is that utility derived from all the items is maximised when it cannot be further enlarged by switching marginal expenditure from some items to others, that is, when the marginal utility of expenditure on all the items is equalised. Thus a government maximises its utility (political, economic or other) from its total expenditure when the last, marginal, million pounds applied to, say, medical research yields no more and no less utility than if it were applied to law and order or the EEC. The special difficulty about all government expenditure, whether on public goods or non-public goods, is that utility cannot easily be measured unless there are prices. A firm maximises the utility (or productivity in this case) from its total expenditure on resources when the marginal ('last') thousand pounds spent on equipment yields no more and no less utility than if it were applied to wages or salaries. Measurement of utility is easier here because the firm loses money if it makes the wrong decision, so it can be assumed that by trial and error it will, in a competitive market, have to learn to make the right decisions. And a family maximises the satisfaction from its total household budget when it equalises its marginal expenditure on food, clothing, drinking, smoking, gambling, entertaining, and even within each category on different kinds of food, clothing, drinking and so on.

The all-important opportunity cost

A perhaps unexpected conclusion is that there is nothing inherently good or bad in any of these goods or services. Although we are accustomed to think of education, medical care, housing and other (usually 'public') services as necessarily good and of many forms of (usually private) expenditure, such as entertaining, drinking, motoring, gambling, or adornment as bad, or at least as self-indulgent, there is no substance in this distinction at all. What matters is the marginal expenditure on each category and how much utility, satisfaction or productivity it could have yielded if it had been spent on something else. It is possible for another million pounds spent by government on 'good' things such as the National Health Service or Council housing to reflect less satisfaction than it would if spent on sports centres or defence or road signs, which may not seem such obviously 'good things'. And a hundred pounds more on warm clothing or even good books may yield a family less satisfaction than if it were spent on motoring, bingo, or fancy footwear. What matters is the alternatives that are foregone – what economists call opportunity costs, one of the most illuminating ideas in economics.

Marginal utility in all government goods and services must be assessed, however crudely, and opportunity cost must still be estimated, however roughly, for government to make decisions. When reductions of £100 million in expenditure on defence are called for, it is implied that the country as a whole, or the people, will derive more satisfaction or utility if the money is spent on, say, education, parks and pleasure grounds, or overseas aid. That may be; but government judgement is based on no specific, real information at all, such as that provided by prices and the real personal opinions and valuations of individual men and women. In practice it is based on hunch, the spurious accuracy of estimates, guesswork, prejudice and calculation of political advantage. Price in open markets is usually more or less imperfect, but in its absence the way is open to decide the use of resources by much more imperfect political influences. Price, at least, reflects the opinions and wishes of the many in the market on how *they* wish to use their resources; in its absence, decisions are taken by the few who gain power in government and who use price not as much as possible but as little as they can by bringing under their control, as 'public' services, a widening range of activities in which there are no prices at all.

Price is fundamental

Not the least essential characteristic of price is that, without it, 'demand' and 'supply' are meaningless. This notion is at first difficult to master. The non-economist is apt to think of the 'demand' for a commodity or service as reflecting a natural state of 'need', a self-evident quantity that requires no explanation. In a world without scarcity, and therefore without opportunity cost (so that using more resources to produce, say, fish would not withdraw resources from producing meat), that would be so. We can also properly talk of 'need' in the sense of a minimum quantity of basic essentials like food or medical care that it is thought no human being should lack. In a Western economy that sense is also permissible, and if a minority of people lack these needs they can and should be provided by others. But in general 'demand' is related to price: the lower the price, the larger the demand, because the less the opportunity costs of other things that are sacrificed. And the lower the price of something, the less of it is supplied, because resources can yield more elsewhere.

The mistaken idea that people have absolute 'needs' originates in the notion that some goods are 'essential' and must be obtained whatever the price. This may be true of some things inside narrow price-ranges within which demand is absolutely 'inelastic'. The demand for milk used in fixed proportions with tea may be inelastic: it does not alter with a change in price (unless the rise is so large that milk is given up).

But the availability of substitutes (made of different quality materials, etc.) makes demand elastic, and it falls perceptibly as price rises. Thus the 'need' for a hospital bed is not fixed. If its cost rises, the individual may prefer a cheaper ward in order to keep up other purchases; and the NHS will similarly reduce quality to keep costs down, as by closing wards or casualty departments. Even in the gruesome example of coffins the demand is not fixed: we all die only once and demand only one; but if they are expensive (that is, require a large sacrifice of other things) cheaper woods or other materials can be used, or *in extremis* shrouds, as prepared for the expected victims of the London blitz. 'Public' services also should be, and have to be, modified as costs change; otherwise the public is being unnecessarily burdened by being compelled to sacrifice alternatives it values more. The danger is that the modifications will be delayed because the government fears unpopularity and loss of parliamentary seats as well as because of compassion for people who would suffer. (This is what has happened in Britain over the cuts in government expenditure that have been under debate in recent years.)

The essential is to grasp that there are not enough resources to satisfy all 'needs', that the use of resources cannot therefore be governed by what are considered 'needs', but must be based on demand backed by purchasing power to indicate the value that people place on various commodities and the sacrifice of other goods they are prepared to make; and that demand is not fixed but varies with price – and is indeed meaningless without reference to price. There is no such thing as 'the demand for' good housing, or hospital beds or teacher-training places, any more than there is a fixed demand for Eccles cakes, toffee apples or tripe and onions. The demand varies with the price. And that is true in Moscow, Warsaw, East Berlin and Peking as well as in Stockholm, Paris, Washington and London. There are no free health services, universities, convalescent homes, bus rides, cinema shows or anything else anywhere.[21]

No such thing as a free health service

If the price of a service is suppressed it must be paid for in some other way. In a society where income and wealth are widely unequal, it may be possible to remove part of the income and wealth from people who have more ('the rich') to provide services 'free' to people with little income and no wealth who could not pay the price ('the poor'). This is the main one of the pretexts used in extending 'free' local government services in the past century, free state education since 1870, in providing partly 'free' (subsidised) housing to several millions since 1915, and in creating the 'free' National Health Service in 1948.

The tragic result is that, as incomes have become more equal, the effects have changed. A transfer of payment from rich to poor made sense. A transfer away from taxpayers with middling (and even less than average) income and back to themselves as *users* of 'free' state services – or even to the better-off, as in higher education and sports amenities – makes nonsense (Part 2). The more they have realised this truth, the more reluctant people have become to pay at all (as tax-payers) even for services they otherwise regard as desirable. And this means that the quality of the social services and benefits they receive is lower than they *could* pay for, and might *want* to pay for in ways they themselves could decide. The 'welfare state' has made us cut off our noses to spite our faces.

This is a most unwelcome – and unexpected – development. And not much help is obtained from restating the case for price-less (or partly 'free') services as transferring payment from people at the times of life when they have more income and wealth to the times when they have less. People as taxpayers stubbornly refuse to see this subtle distinction. And if this is what they want to do, they do not have to do it through the state. They simply do not like paying taxes at *any* times of their lives. They object not to the tax-rates, the tax-base, or the tax-locale (central taxes, National insurance, VAT, local rates) but to the tax-take. They simply are fed up with someone else spending their money for them.

Why? This obstinacy seems puzzling. It may appear especially mulish when the tax payments are made for services that seem obviously desirable like education, medical care, housing, transport, fire protection, refuse collection, and so on. Some perplexed people refuse to believe it. 'I have long believed,' said a former Minister, 'that if the people understand what they get for their taxes they are less likely to argue against them.' (Mr Eric Heffer, *The Times*, 12 March 1976.) It is impossible to demonstrate that he is wrong, but until he proves he is right his opinion sounds like wishful thinking. It is not a view he can claim to be true until it is proved false. Governments of all parties have since the war asked the people to pay higher taxes for more or better social benefits for all and sundry. Increasing tax avoidance and evasion show they would rather not. And politicians of all parties are at last accepting the evidence.

Why will people pay less in taxes for 'free' services than they could pay, and might prefer to pay, in other ways? Why are 'free' British state welfare services less good than priced welfare services might be?

Paying by charges or taxes

The solution is not difficult to see. It requires only an unsentimental, though not unworthy, view of human nature – the reactions of men as husbands, women as wives, and both as parents. It can be wrapped up in jargon as economic theory but it can be put in plain English: *ordinary people will pay more for a service if they can see their families will benefit than they will in taxes for a service in which they can see no benefit for higher tax-payment.*

It is this realistic reading of human nature that reveals the inappropriateness of taxes as the method of paying for personal welfare services. It is not a theory or a hunch, or a cynical view of human selfishness. It is a description which realistically captures, without illusion or humbug, the attitude of ordinary men and women all over the world, under all economic systems, capitalist, socialist or communist. And it is what the exceptional politician of perception and integrity sees, and says, when he tries in the real world to run social policies based on the unworldly assumption that men and women are far-seeing saints. In 1967, after two and a half years as Minister coordinating the social services, Mr Douglas (now Lord) Houghton said:

> While people would be willing to pay for better health services for themselves, they may not be willing to pay more in taxes as a kind of insurance premium which may bear no relation to the services they receive.[42]

And in 1969, after two years as Minister for Social Services, the late Richard Crossman, who was too much of a scholar to blur the truth as he found it, signed a White Paper on National Superannuation which said:

> ... people are prepared to subscribe more in a contribution for their own personal or family security than they would be willing to pay in taxation devoted to a wide variety of different purposes.

Self-interest and selfishness

The British are not callous or ungenerous: they pay taxes willingly to help people who, through old age, disability or other causes, cannot help themselves;[103] and they work for and give money to good causes, their neighbours in trouble, the local hospital or school, the old people's home, their church. But they object to helping people who can help themselves. Where there are two ways of paying for a service (taxes and prices) and one way (taxes) gives no benefit to themselves, they prefer to pay in ways (prices) that do.

That is hardly surprising. It is, however, disappointing to many who hoped that people would willingly go on paying in taxes for communal causes. That is the assumption behind the welfare state common in all political parties. But it requires a decision by each man or woman to put the benefits to his family second to the consequences to others, including strangers of whom he may not approve. That degree of self-sacrifice may be expected from uncommon individuals, or in wartime or other crises. But why should we suppose that people would be better human beings if they put causes they do not know before causes they do? Because we have confused self-interest with selfishness.

The better arrangement is to avoid the conflict between a man's family and outside interests and try to guide him to serve the general interest, which he cannot know, by serving his family or personal causes, which he does know. He is moved to serve his personal or local causes not by selfishness but by knowledge.

The apparently simple question, whether to pay by market prices or to suppress them and pay by taxes, thus raises deep philosophic issues. But the question must be answered by citizens and their representatives in a democracy; and it must be answered all the sooner if an error in reasoning is preventing people from paying as much as they could and would, and therefore producing services that are inferior to those they wish to have. When the services include education, health, housing and other basic services, we must give the matter urgent thought, and reverse policies shown to be undesirable.

The reigning error

Happily such reconsideration has begun. At long last, after years of irresponsible overspending by Conservative and Labour governments, both central and local, anxiety about government expenditure and the urgency of making cuts spread to people in almost all schools of thought and all the major political parties. But the right solution will not be adopted until all these groups and sub-groups recognise a fundamental flaw in British thinking on social policy.

The error lies in the three-stage argument at the beginning of this chapter.

1 All people should have the minimum essentials for civilised living;
2 their incomes are sometimes too low to pay for them;
3 therefore they should be provided free by the state, and not only to people with low incomes but to everyone.

The first stage is accepted by everyone. The second is self-evident. The fatal flaw lies in the third stage. It simply does not follow from the first two.

We may differ about the meaning of minimum. We may differ about how often incomes are too low, and about the cause; whether the low incomes are unavoidable and what can be done to make them large enough. But what should not have been accepted – certainly after World War II – is the conclusion that the state therefore had to supply services wholly free, or partly free at prices reduced by subsidies. This error has misled all British governments for a century to create a vast unnecessary structure of free education, almost wholly

free medical care, partly free housing; free libraries, museums, art
galleries; free 'personal' social services such as home helps and meals
in the home; free or largely free local health services such as health
centres, midwifery, home nursing, vaccination and immunisation, ambulances and family planning; (almost) free police and fire services;
free sewerage; free recreational and sports facilities; free roads, partly
free (subsidised) parking; free employment agencies (now called Job
Centres); free environmental services – parks, public conveniences,
town and country planning, allotments; subsidised private street
works, etc. etc. Much of this structure was unnecessary; it is increasingly undesirable; and it can be changed.

Abe Lincoln didn't live here

All the services that happen to have been taken over by government,
local or national, are described as 'public'. This is a highly misleading
term. It can mean, first, that they are, in Abraham Lincoln's words,
'of' the people (that is, decided by them), run 'by' the people, or 'for'
(the benefit of) the people. None of these claims is self-evident. Second,
it can mean that all these services are 'public' in the sense that they
differ in a fundamental way from 'private' services. This claim is not
true either.

Of the people?

Which 'public services' arise out of public wishes?

There is no systematic mechanism in Britain for recording public
opinion on any single 'public' service. When did anyone in Britain
have the opportunity to record a vote for or against the National
Health Service? or Council housing? or public libraries? or public golf
courses? Apart from the referendum on the Common Market in June
1975 no one has ever been able to say 'Yes' or 'No' to any single
political question. Your opinion is sought through your representatives
– in Parliament or Councils – on twenty, thirty or ninety issues at
once. But that is a very imperfect second-best. It means that everyone
must accept (or at least pay for) the 'public' services supported by the
political party or group with the largest number of votes. If there are
more than two groups, one group can compel the *majority* of us to
accept what the group with the largest *minority* wants to do. That has
been the situation in Britain for many years. In October 1974 the
group elected was supported by less than two in five of those who

bothered to vote (or not much more than one in four of all citizens with votes). Indeed, since the war no government of any party has had a majority of the votes cast, still less of the votes that could have been cast (Table A).

There is, then, no way in which any one 'public' service can be isolated and supported or opposed. We must support or oppose all the proposals offered by each party or group. And this means that if a proposal for, say, the National Health Service is made by *all* groups, we have no choice at all: no way of opposing it or escaping from it once it is implemented – except by emigrating, which some people have preferred. Moreover, if the representatives take it into their heads after they have reached Parliament or the Council to make another service public – say, theatres, or fire insurance, or medicines, or tourism, or banking or bingo – there is nothing we can do about it. In this way they can depart a long way from the wishes of the *real* public who are the sovereign people with the power (on paper) to decide what we think should or should not be made 'public': for it is we who benefit or suffer, and not least, it is we who pay.

Any idea should, of course, have a chance of being tried *at the expense of private individuals*, but the British political system gives individual political activists the chance to foist a new 'public' service on the public, at *its* expense, and on a national scale which destroys for years and years the chance to reverse it if it fails.

By the people?

Are the 'public' services run by the people? On paper the people are represented by MPs and local Councillors who reflect their opinions. In practice the reality is very different. Representatives may be opinionated, self-willed autocrats who say one thing on party platforms or in election addresses and do another after being elected. Even if they were all upright, conscientious servants of the people, they are not elected as spokesmen on this, that and the other, but as men who in principle reflect the general approach of the people and apply it to unforeseeable circumstances as they emerge. And even though they must represent their electors on collective services, such as protection against world or internal disorder, they cannot represent each individual elector in a personal service.

This is the basic weakness of controlling education, medical care or many other services, through 'representatives'. Ministers and politicians know first-hand from their party officials, stalwarts and activists what they think individuals in the party, or even outside it, think about public goods, but they cannot know their private feelings and wishes as husbands and wives, parents and children, in personal services. No representative in, say, education can represent hundreds of parents, who know the characters and temperaments, the feelings and anxieties, of their children better than anyone else. Much the same applies to most of the personal benefits in the public services. It is unrealistic to suppose that politicians (even if saints) and officials (even if geniuses) can know as much as millions of men and women who have to adapt themselves to unforeseen, changing conditions. And politicians are not saints, nor officials geniuses.

Even when politicians and officials do their best to provide good schools, hospitals, and so on, the man whose wife is not comfortable in the hospital ward or the parent whose child is not happy in the school cannot change conditions except by the lengthy business of persuading hundreds or thousands or millions of other husbands and parents, a task which daunts most, especially the inarticulate. Such services are therefore innately impersonal, unresponsive and conservative; they are bureaucratic rather than democratic. They bend to political muscle, personal connections, social influence, individual pressure or bullying. What ordinary, quiet, uninfluential people want is a method by which they themselves, by private *individual* action, can influence conditions quietly and without confrontation, voice-raising, marches, public meetings, petitions, deputations, or any other kind of public fuss. What they want is simply a means of exit to another hospital or school. Such methods are available (Chapters 4 to 9), but they are not made part of the machinery of 'public' services in Britain. Politicians on the hustings claim it serves the public, but in real life it dissuades or stops the people from trying something else if they are dissatisfied.

For the people?

Are public services run for the people? It is again impossible to tell, for by definition public services cannot be compared with alternatives, which on the contrary may be outlawed – as in transport, fuel, postal services, etc. If government were really efficient in satisfying the people, it would provide easy ways for them to try alternative services, so that it would be clear for all to see beyond dispute whether the people preferred public to alternative services. But this is precisely what government does not do. Politicians characteristically abhor competition; unlike nature they prefer a vacuum.

So we must take with a large pinch of salt the notion that 'public' services are necessarily in the public interest. Simply calling them public, or talking about public accountability through Parliament or the local Council, is not enough.

'Externalities' and 'free rides'

The previous chapter discussed the characteristic which marks off what are truly public goods from those that are really private services in disguise – that public goods have to be supplied for everyone or no one and cannot be withheld from people who choose to take a 'free ride'. This special characteristic of public goods makes it necessary (or at least desirable) to organise them through government and to finance them by taxes – in short to nationalise (or municipalise) them.

The difference is clear enough in principle but it may be difficult to work in practice, because many goods and services shed benefits to outsiders or third parties who cannot (technically or economically) be charged for them. In this sense almost every human activity yields what economists call 'external benefits'. A man who plants sweet-smelling flowers benefits his neighbours, and if he wears button-holes he may please both friends and strangers; but he could not charge them fees to help him pay for his seeds. If we all considered the feelings of neighbours and strangers we should increase happiness all round. But it does not follow that we should transform all private individuals into public services, or even regulate all private activities by political devices. For we might lose the other benefits of individual choice, variety and initiative if we had government subsidies and inspectors to ensure that everyone's garden grew flowers that pleased all neighbours. There could be no end to that process of maximising externalities. We should all be living in one another's pockets. So in practice public goods are confined to those whose external benefits are clearly and considerably larger than the costs and defects of state control, and where there is no economic method of financing them except by taxes.

In practice 'public services' has become a political term, almost an advertising or public relations label, used for all the services that have gradually, down the years since the mid-nineteenth century, been

gathered together under government for all sorts of reasons, willy-nil-
ly. It conveys the impression that they must all be organised by
government and that they are all necessarily in the public interest.
That is a myth. They need not be. And they are not.

Charging for choice

They do not all have to be organised by government and financed by
taxes. Some could be financed by prices. They are not all necessarily
in the public interest. Some could be organised outside government.
This possibility opens up new vistas of wider choices for users of services, competition between suppliers, and a wider variety of methods
of payment.

If services now supplied by government can and should be financed
by prices – charges, fees etc. – the chances are that people who pay
prices will want the same feeling of personal choice that they now
have in purchasing family and household goods and services – food,
clothing, furniture, books and newspapers, motoring, holidaying, and
so on. They will look around for suppliers who can give them the
choice that national or local government cannot, or does not. That is
where the old thinking – that only the state can or should supply what
are now called 'public services' – will have to give way to 'new
thinking' – that a service should be provided by *any* supplier, state or
private, who can supply it in the form that most pleases the customer.
But that is a long and exciting story that must wait for Part II. If the
main purpose is to satisfy people as individuals a lot of established
myths and charades will have to be abandoned. Not least of them is
the notion that government introduces a new service only when it is
required by the people and ends it when it is no longer wanted. The
myth that 'public' services are necessarily a good thing has made them
seem sacrosanct; they must not be touched whatever new requirements arise, or whatever new circumstances are brought by
technical and social change. No one may say a word against 'free'
public baths and wash houses that go back to 1846, or 'free' public
libraries that go back to 1850, or 'free' refuse collection that goes back
to 1875 – despite the enormous changes in the last century and a half.
Yet, for public men who represent the people, to refuse to change
anything when circumstances change is itself a public dis-service.

3 Private "public" services

The great debate has at last begun over how to cut inflated government expenditure. But it will not be resolved as long as it continues to ignore the extent to which 'public' services are not public goods at all but yield private benefits that could and should be paid for by price. And it will not be resolved so long as we think only of re-arranging the government machinery by which cuts are made from on high by politicians.

This debate will not lead to the right solution so long as people who at long last joined it, tardily, like the late Mr Anthony Crosland, argue that cuts in government expenditure may be desirable as a temporary necessity to fight off inflation (by increasing production and shifting resources into industrial investment and exports) but are not based on a permanent principle.[18]

What is at stake is very much a permanent principle. It is the true principle, perhaps new to politicians but not to economists, that public goods should be financed by public methods (taxes) but private benefits where possible by private methods (prices). And it must replace the false notion that any activity or function that government has happened to gather to itself for a rag-bag of reasons, good or bad, still valid or wildly out of date, sensible or nonsensical, shall all be christened 'public' services and financed by taxes whether or not this is the way to efficiency, economy, equity, choice or democracy.

A permanent principle

Shedding the old principle will not be easy for men and women in all schools of thought and parties, Conservative, Liberal or Labour. The debate will be abortive unless Social Democrats like Mr. Roy Jenkins recognise the new principle. Others like Mr. David Marquand[64] and Professor Lord Vaizey[115] seem to have done so, or at least moved towards it. Paternalistic Liberals and Tories, no less than paternalistic Labourites, will have to abandon the wrong principle and accept the true one. It is a permanent principle because government expenditure is in large part wrongly financed by taxes, and therefore will not be cut as it should be – by informed consumers rather than by uninformed politicians – until it is financed by charges. No insuperable technical or political obstacles stand in the way. The adoption of the true principle could transform and reinvigorate British society in a decade. That is the solution for which this book argues.

In 1974 the total national output of goods and services was around £75 billion (a billion in this book is a thousand million). The figure is growing – because of inflation rather than economic efficiency – but we are more concerned about the *proportions* in which it is divided between public goods and private benefits, which will remain much the same until policy is changed from taxing to pricing. About £25 billion, or a third, was produced directly by government (national, regional or local), by government employees and equipment in government offices, factories, mines, quarries, generating stations, ordnance depots, barracks, railways, buses, coaches, abattoirs, schools, hospitals, universities, more offices, job centres, libraries, museums, art galleries, health centres, ambulances, children's residential homes, homes for the elderly, prisons, police stations, fire stations, law courts, sewage farms, water reservoirs, refuse vans, swimming and washing baths, town halls, roads, parks, car parks, tennis courts, golf courses, theatres and yet more offices.

In addition to the third of the total national output directly produced by government, it also decides the disposal of a further fifth of the national income. This part is returned in cash, in family allowances, grants of various kinds, pensions and so on, for people to spend as they wish (subject, even then, to taxes on their purchases). Government thus directly controls the production and the distribution of a third of the national output and then indirectly decides who shall receive a further fifth of national purchasing power. In this sense it controls over half the national economy. And in so far as taxes have the same effect on production, incentives, costs of collection, avoidance, evasion and so on whether they are returned in goods and services or in money, it is correct to think of the government controlling over half, not one-third, of the national product.

Public goods proper

For readers who like to think in figures, the tables that follow show the broad orders of magnitude at a glance. Table B arranges all the main items of government expenditure into five broad groups, not rigidly defined but overlapping at the edges. Group I contains the more or less 'pure' public goods which yield common benefits to all, and which cannot be separately organised by each person, family, or household. This group accounts for about 15 per cent of total government expenditure and 8 per cent of GNP. It is essentially the hard core of unavoidable government functions. Even here one or two of the smaller items, such as land drainage or law courts, may contain private benefits that could be separated and charged for.

Public services with some separable private benefits

Group II contains services familiarly supplied by local or regional (county) government, usually without charge, but containing some benefits that are or could be rendered to individuals and financed by charging. Roads, police, fire and other services are discussed in later chapters. This group accounts for about 14 per cent of government expenditure (8 per cent of GNP). The 'public corporations' are included here because transport and fuel are sometimes regarded as 'social services' that should not charge prices that will cover costs but should be financed partly by taxes. Mr Sidney Weighall, the General Secretary of the National Union of Railwaymen, has vividly maintained that the railways should no more be expected to pay for themselves than aircraft carriers. He saw no difference. The difference is that aircraft carriers are public goods; railways are not.

Separable private benefits

Group III contains services that have also been supplied by local, regional or national government, some for a century or more, some for only a quarter of a century, but which largely comprise separable benefits. It may be surprising to say this of education and medical care, although it is obviously true of housing. Unfortunately, although 'housing' is a clear enough description of houses or flats or other forms of living space, 'education' is a technical term that covers a wide range of services from public goods to purely personal benefits. So does 'the National Health Service' which I shall argue (Chapter 5) is a dog's breakfast of a term that is both too wide and too narrow to describe the services designed to maintain or restore health. Group III accounts for about 40 per cent of government expenditure, and 22 per cent of GNP.

TABLE B: WHERE OUR MONEY GOES: Government expenditure in 1974

	Total expenditure (£million)	Proportion of total government expenditure (£41,600)	Proportion of gross national product (£74,000)
I Public goods with inseparable benefits (charging impracticable or uneconomic)			
Military defence	4,221	10	6
Civil defence	14	•	•
External relations (embassies, missions, EEC, etc.)	654	2	1
Parliament & law courts	221	1	•
Prisons	149	•	•
Public health	101	•	•
Land drainage & coast protection	69	•	•
Finance & tax collection	496	1	1
Other government services	166	•	•
	6,091	15	8
II Public goods with some separable benefits (charging partly practicable)			
Government (central & local) and 'public' corporation current & capital expentiture	2,429	6	3
Roads and public lighting	1,195	3	2
Research	326	1	•
Parks, pleasure grounds, etc.	265	1	•
Local government services ('misc')	700	2	1
Police	706	2	1
Fire services	169	•	•
Records, registration, surveys	38	•	•
	5,828	14	8

	Total expenditure (£million)	Proportion of total government expenditure (£41,600)	Proportion of gross national product (£74,000)
III Substantially or wholly separable benefits (charging substantially practicable)			
Education	4,864	12	7
National Health Service	3,819	9	5
Personal social services	677	2	1
School meals, milk & welfare foods	282	1	*
Employment service	268	1	*
Libraries, museums & art galleries	222	1	*
Housing	3,942	9	5
Water, sewage, refuse disposal	730	2	1
Transport & communications	1,894	5	3
	16,698	40	22
IV Subsidies, grants, pensions and other (mostly) cash disbursements			
Agriculture, forestry, fishing, food	1,049	3	1
Cash benefits for social insurance etc.	6,845	16	9
Miscellaneous subsidies, grants, lending, etc. to private/personal sector	1,363	3	2
	9,257	22	13
V Interest on National Debt	3,732	9	6
TOTAL GOVERNMENT EXPENDITURE	41,606	100	56

Source: The figures are from the National Income Blue Book, 1974.
    The classification into groups is mine.

* Less than one per cent

Cash raised in taxes and returned

Group IV contains tax monies paid back in cash benefits to taxpayers, often the very same people: about 22 per cent of government expenditure. These are the 'transfer payments'.

National debt interest is shown separately as Group V.

Public corporations?

The 'public' corporations are mostly the familiar nationalised industries, the Post Office, coal, electricity, gas, airways, railways and buses – housing and new towns. At this point we may again note the repeated use of the misleading term 'public'. This is a political term that does not indicate a real economic distinction. Neither general reasoning nor experience supports the insinuation that public corporations are necessarily 'in the public interest', in contrast with private industry which it is implied, is not in the public interest because it works for private profit. There is a confusion here between purpose and result. It may be the *intention* of Parliament that public corporations shall work only for the public interest. It does not follow that the intention is fulfilled in practice. But more than that: whether or not their intention matters morally to the real 'public' (the users and consumers of nationalised fuel and transport) what certainly does matter to them is the *result* – whether they receive good value for their (private) money. Obversely, whether or not private capitalists work only for personal profit, what matters to the user of privately-produced food, clothing, homes, books, entertainment, motoring, etc., is the result: good value or not. And, in this result, the question whether government producers are financed by prices from customers or by taxes from politicians is very much one that should be, but is hardly ever, asked.

Since the late 1960's these 'public' industries and services have been required to cover their costs, though not necessarily in every single year. In practice we know that the railways, air, steel and others are constantly asking for government grants (taken from the taxpayer) or loans to cover losses. And even if, in any one year, one of them has covered its costs as a whole, there is internal 'cross-subsidising' of some services by others. For some years the telephones have been subsidising the parcels services, the Inter-City train traveller has been subsidising the outer commuter working in London, and so on. How much sense does that make?

Private benefits: public money

To discuss the extent to which government services could be paid for by prices, I have shown in Table C the expenditure on local government services for the latest year available, and the income drawn in fees, charges and sales. (Later figures will show much the same story until charges are made or raised.) I have then calculated how much of the total expenditure is financed from prices paid by the users of the services and how much by the ratepayer and taxpayer, who may use them little or not at all.

These official figures will, I imagine, shock some readers. The most surprising item is that only half of the expenditure on what is openly and officially called *private* 'street and other works' is evidently paid for by charges levied on the people for whom the work is done; the rest is paid for by taxes extracted from other people who do not benefit from the work, at least directly and obviously (further discussed below). Then again car-parking, a convenience for the individual motorist, drew less than two-thirds of its expenditure from charges; the rest was paid by local taxpayers who did not park, who may indeed not own cars, or who may prefer to keep cars out of their shopping areas or even altogether out of their towns, suburbs or villages. And so on: homes for the elderly had a third of their costs paid by charges, allotments less than a quarter, swimming and washing baths and laundries just over a fifth. In each of the rest the proportion was under a fifth, in many under a tenth, and in some (including the largest, such as education and health) 5 per cent or less. These are averages for the country as a whole. For individual local authorities the gap between expenditure and charges in car-parking, sports facilities, housing and other services may be even more.

Externalities and absurdities

In some of these services it could be argued, and is argued by some economists, sociologists and politicians, that the benefit was not only personal to the user but spilled over to other people, so that it was right for part, most, or all of the cost to be borne by third parties, or by people in general on their rates or taxes. In principle that argument is right: perhaps passers-by are pleased by the private 'street and other

TABLE C: HOW MUCH WE PAY FOR LOCAL GOVERNMENT SERVICES BY CHARGES AND BY TAXES

	Expenditure (£million)	Income from fees & charges and sales[1] (£ million)	Charges etc. as % of expenditure	Remainder paid by taxes[2] (%)
1 'Rate fund' services (current expenditure)				
Education:				
Nursery	10	*	*	100
Primary	839	9	1	99
Secondary	1,073	35	3	97
Special	131	15	11	89
Further: Polytechnics & Regional colleges	127	12	9	91
Colleges of art	17	1	8	92
Agricultural	10	2	18	82
Other major colleges, etc.	294	36	12	88
Evening institutes	22	4	19	81
Other	206	72	35	65
Teacher training	127	4	3	97
School health	46	*	1	99
Recreation & social & physical training				
Youth	29	1	2	98
Adults, etc.	13	1	7	93
Other education services	6	*	6	94
School meals, milk, etc.	294	100	34	66
Libraries	95	5	6	94
Museums and art galleries	11	1	5	95
Health:				
Health centres	9	1	8	92
Mother/children clinics etc.	22	1	6	94
Midwifery	18	*	1	99
Visitors	21	*	*	100
Home nursing	35	*	*	100
Vaccination & immunisation	4	*	*	100
Ambulance	62	1	2	98
Prevention of illness	15	*	3	97
Family Planning	6	1	1	99
Personal social services				
Residential care	249	66	26	74
Day care — day nurseries (incl. play groups)	15	2	12	88
Community care:				
Home helps (incl. laundry)	55	3	5	95
Meals in the home	6	1	18	82
Other	37	1	2	98
Police	530	19	4	96
Fire	123	2	2	98
Justice (courts, petty sessions, probation)	56	1	2	98

Source of figures: *Local Government Financial Statistics, England and Wales, 1973—4,* HMSO, 1975.

* Less than £1 million or 1 per cent

1 Sales are of miscellaneous used vehicles and equipment, publications, agricultural produce, waste paper, etc.

	Expenditure (£million)	Income from fees & charges and sales[1] (£million)	Charges etc. as % of expenditure	Remainder paid by taxes[2] (%)
Sewerage	242	15	6	94
Refuse	167	11	7	93
Baths (swimming & washing) & laundries	49	13	26	74
Land drainage, flood prevention	33	1	4	96
Smallholdings	6	1	12	88
Sea fisheries, pest control etc.	7	2	27	63
Roads: Highways	471	12	3	97
Public lighting	48	1	2	98
Vehicle parking	33	20	60	40
Youth employment	10	*	*	100
Sheltered employment and workshops	8	3	41	59
Environment				
Parks and open spaces	131	11	8	92
National and countryside parks	4	*	1	99
Town & country planning	115	5	4	96
Housing (other than below — 2)	282	18	6	94
Public conveniences	20	*	2	98
Air pollution prevention	6	*	*	100
Other health measures	46	2	5	95
River pollution prevention	4	*	*	100
Allotments	2	*	23	77
Private street etc. works	20	10	51	49
Registration of births, etc.	6	2	35	65
Civil defence	2	*	1	99
Coast protection	5	*	*	100
2 Housing (current expenditure 'revenue account')	1,231	740	60	40
3 'Trading services'				
Water	208	174	84	16
Passenger transport	90	76	84	16
Cemeteries & crematoria	20	7	35	65
Fishing harbours	0.4	0.2	61	39
Other ports & piers	14	12	88	12
Civic restaurants	4	4	88	12
Markets horticultural	3	1	39	61
others	15	8	55	45
Slaughterhouses	6	3	55	45
Aerodromes	20	12	63	37
Industrial estates	11	2	20	80
District heating schemes	0.5	0.4	83	17
Corporation estates	31	4	15	85

2 The true balance of expenditure paid by the taxpayer (and ratepayer) is in some items higher than shown in the last column because the figures for income from fees and charges include sums paid by local authorities in other areas, not by direct private consumers or users (for example, fees for children at boarding schools).

works' as they pass by and don't snap at their children when they reach home. The benefits of car-parking spill over to pedestrian shoppers who have fewer cars to avoid in the streets, to shopkeepers whose sales may rise, to out-of-town car-borne shoppers attracted by free or subsidised car-parking, to ratepayers in general whose rates are lower than they otherwise would be because shopkeepers' rates are higher, to enthusiasts for clean buildings because shopkeepers paint their shop-fronts more frequently, to the local church, old people's homes and hospitals which receive more gifts from better-off traders, and so on without end.

This line of reasoning – that individual activity affects the community by its 'externalities' – is strongly argued by sociologists who tend to see all life as communal and by politicians who naturally rather like to think that the state could run human activity better than short-sighted, blinkered individuals could do for themselves. But all the same it reduces logic to absurdity. It ends with the conclusion that *everything* we do – from eating and drinking to queueing and waiting – affects everybody else, that nothing we do is personal or private, and therefore *every* activity should be financed by taxes and directed by government officials. This, of course, is the recipe for the all-in, comprehensive, totalitarian society. No country that hoped to maintain any personal liberties could go as far as that, even if some efficiency in using resources was lost by maintaining individual decisions.

But more than that. Even if the externality argument made sense it would merely show that the liberty to make individual decisions has costs, *not that the costs are too high to pay*. This is the key to understanding the fallacy of the argument that supposed or conjectured externalities – like the social good that it is thought will be done by university graduates – are sufficient to make the case for subsidising the producer (students in this case) at the expense of everyone else who is supposed to benefit. In conception we may all do (unintended) good to everyone else, but it produces no basis for policy. The externalities would have to be measured much more precisely by an army of calculators, estimators, assessors and adjudicators; a vast structure of subsidies from everyone to everyone else would have to be calculated by more officials; still more officials would have to be recruited to pay them; more taxes would have to be raised to finance them; and more tax-gatherers would be required to collect the taxes. There would be fewer of us left to produce the income and wealth to yield the subsidies and the taxes, and we should all end up leaning on one another. In short, even if the externalities could be identified and measured, the cost of transferring the subsidies from everyone to everyone else would in the end exceed the benefits.

We can go even further than that. Individual initiative that does not need official permission also has external benefits – in stimulating innovation, change, abandonment of old attitudes and institutions, economic advance. Progress might be largely stillborn if innovation were closely regulated even by a benevolent state, as it was in the guild system of mediaeval England, as it now is by authoritarian states in Eastern Europe, Asia and Africa, and as some politicians would like in Britain today. This totalitarian policy would throw out the baby with the bath water. Rather than try to calculate all the remote and indefinable public benefits that could flow from private action, we must work the other way round and assess what proportion of 'public' services consists of separable benefits to particular individuals who could be identified and who could be made to pay for them.

This is sometimes a very difficult task. No one knows the exclusive, separable personal benefit in a 'public' service for which individuals would pay rather than go without. The reason is simply that they have never had to pay for it: there has been no 'market'. The only way to find out is by the characteristically British method of trial and error. And, to begin the process of thinking in this unknown territory, it is a refreshing exercise to start from scratch and consider each service to see how far it yields personal benefits that could be paid for in prices. We can then discuss how much should remain paid for by taxes.

We are leaving aside for the moment the plausible reasons why many activities have been made 'public' services – poverty, irresponsibility, economy, monopoly – and also the less reputable reasons like political aggrandisement and civil-service empire-building. (They are discussed in Chapters 10 to 12). Here we consider only the extent to which 'public' services yield separable personal benefits for which people could pay.

How far are 'public' services public goods?

'Public' services are supplied by three agencies: central government, the public corporations, and local government. ('Agencies' is a good word: it reminds us that, at least on paper, they are not authorities over the people, but their 'agents': not independent principals but employees.) In practice public services are run by politicians who go their own way and civil servants whose power as disobedient servants was vividly suggested by the late Richard Crossman's account of Departments that generated their own policies, consulted opposite numbers in other Departments to thwart difficult Ministers, and behaved like an independent authority of able, well-intentioned but still irresponsible autocrats who act as judge and jury on what is administratively practicable, and who, without much knowledge of public wishes at all, offer advice on what is 'politically possible'. [19]

The agency that supplies the largest element of real public goods like defence is the central government (Group I, Table B). But it also supplies a surprisingly high proportion of separable private benefits (Groups II and III).

Defence: Defence against external enemies is clear enough. There is no known way of making people pay for it by private fees, or at least no way that is economic. Even if it were possible to calculate the risks from destruction of life, liberty or property from aerial attack or invasion in different locations, and the value of individual lives, liberty and property saved by efficient defence, it is impossible to confine defence to people who pay. And for such services, at least for the forseeable future, all must agree to pay collectively by taxes, though individuals may supplement collective provision (below). Perhaps one day, if technical development makes the defence of small groups possible, 'fees' may become practicable, as some brighter younger American economists persist in discussing. [23, 97, 98, 99]

Civil defence: Much the same goes for civil defence, since the damage caused by modern nuclear weapons is widespread. Even so, people will supplement whatever defences they finance jointly through taxes by coming together and combining in small groups to reduce (by blast-proofing, laying in stores, etc) loss of life and damage to possessions from localised weapons or warfare. And no government can stop them, even though they do so unequally.

External relations: External relations seem a clear case of a public good that benefits all citizens (or, if they are not conducted wisely, a public bad from which all suffer). The benefit may not be equal but it is not easily separable or traceable to individuals or local groups and so cannot be paid for by charging. Even so, services to individuals or firms may be.

Parliament: Parliament is another public good (or bad). Its law-making affects us all; and we cannot easily be charged as individuals for the benefits we have had from (or compensated for the harm done by) the externalities of nineteenth and twentieth century politicians or governments. Shakespeare knew about externalities when he said: 'The evil that men do lives after them, the good is oft interred with their bones.'

Justice: The law courts seem another obvious public good that must be paid for by taxes. Yet the settlement of disputes over agreements and contracts does not have to be done by government officials. It is possible to conceive of private arbitration and even courts, strange though that may sound. Some American economists are ahead of us[23, 97, 98, 99] in developing these ideas.

Prisons: Prisons are another obvious public good that cannot be paid for by pricing (though prisoners could pay for their keep by working, and perhaps compensate people they have wronged). It does not follow that prisons are best conducted by government officials; but that – the whole question of the difference between government and private management, even of public goods – is a subject for a separate book.

Public health: These are the environmental and preventive activities (such as treating polluted water and other sources of infection, or supervising disease-carrying overseas visitors) that benefit us all. Even here we can be charged for some, like inoculations. (A common mistake is to suppose that *all* health services are public.)

Public goods with some separable private services

So much for the main public goods in Group I. All the direct government services in Group II – roads, research, parks and pleasure grounds, 'miscellaneous local government services' (perhaps sports and recreational facilities are tucked away here: they are not shown separately), police and fire services – have services supplied jointly. But equally obviously they all render, or could render, services that are individual and separable, though possibly to a lesser extent. And to this extent they could be financed by charges.

The reader accustomed to thinking of them as public services may be surprised, but I would ask him or her to recall that charging is being advocated because it is a better method of financing some services than is taxing. The scope for pricing local government services is discussed in Chapters 7 and 8.

The public corporations provide services like fuel, transport and telephones, that could be financed largely or wholly by charging but often are not. They are discussed in Chapter 9.

Public services with substantially separable private benefits

No less is this true of the welfare or social services in Group III.

Education: There are clearly personal separable services in education. In Australia the parents of one child in four pay fees. In Britain fees are paid for one child in twenty in addition to taxes for state education that some parents prefer not to use. This is not solely because of higher income but partly from preference; not all fee-payers are wealthy. In Australia parents who want to pay fees have been helped by being allowed to deduct fees, fares and other school costs from taxable income.

Health: In medical care also charges are conceivable, feasible and practicable, as has been seen in prescription, appliance and other charges in Britain, and as is clear from the practice of every other English-speaking and West European country, none of which has followed Britain in financing health services (almost wholly) by taxes. They use a variety of charges financed by a mixture of social and private insurance, and a mixture of voluntary insurance with com-pulsory insurance for basic and major ('catastrophic') health risks.

Personal social services: Personal social services (the official description) hardly require further argument: they are separable by definition. The confusion here has been between poverty and medical incapacity. Poverty is not a reason for 'free' supply: people with low income can be enabled to pay by 'topping up' their income. Neither is incapacity a reason for 'free' supply, but for 'topping up' the low in-comes of incapacitated people. Here an important principle in social policy is much misunderstood. We help people not because they are old, or disabled, or widowed, or for any other physical or social deficiency, but where old age, disability or some other handicap prevents them from earning enough to pay. By no means all the old or incapacitated or widowed are poor; and the more help they receive the less is left for those who are.

Other public services with private benefits: Employment services, libraries, museums and the arts, sports and recreational amenities, housing, water, sewage, refuse disposal, transport: there is no technical obstacle in the way of supplying these personal separable services and financing them at least partly if not largely by charges. Then why are charges not used? What are the obstacles? That is the subject of Part III. But before that we discuss possible methods of charging and the advantages of doing so in Part II.

PART 2

You Pays Your Taxes, But You Gets No Choice

4 Education: paying for consumer power

One of the most important elements in the vast structure of so-called public services that, like Topsy, has 'just growed' for a hundred years or more is education. State education has been created according to policies decided by central government, executed largely by local government, and financed by both with little heed to the preferences of mothers and fathers. Little wonder that politicians (Conservative as well as Labour), officials and teachers point to the incapacity of parents, and even lack of interest in education, as reasons for resisting efforts to give them more influence and authority in the curricula and conduct of British schools. Circular reasoning could hardly be more evident: parents cannot choose schools; therefore we will continue with the system that discourages them from learning how to choose.

In 1977 there is still little sign that the education pundits see the inconsistency in their claim that state paternalism must continue for ever more. They can hardly concede that family paternalism would not have tolerated the recent deterioration in tax-financed state schools and standards recognised, at long last, by a Labour Prime Minister. Good teachers will privately agree; their trade union officials and politicians will blithely talk of raising standards by continuing the old attitude of keeping parents out by not encouraging them into state schools. If parents had paid fees they would have made a fuss long before now.

Since 1870 education has increasingly been supplied more or less 'free' by the state. To put it more honestly, it has been paid for increasingly by more and more of us through rates and taxes rather than by prices. Why? Were taxes the only way of paying for it? Are they now the best way?

This will be a fairly long chapter because it discusses general principles – in particular the objections to charging, choice and competition – that apply also to other public services. The following chapters on health, housing and others are accordingly shorter.

Not public goods

Most of us in Britain have never paid for education – directly. But as
the lengthening list and rising costs of 'free' goods and services require
more taxes to be paid by people with middling and lower incomes as
the wealthier are taxed to the limit, more and more of us are coming to
know that payment must be made in the end by no one but ourselves.
(The figures come in Chapter 10.)

But perhaps there is no other way? Perhaps, whether paying by taxes is the best way or not, it is the only *practicable* way and we must
accept it whatever its disadvantages? That is not true. All forms of
formal education, from nursery to adult, can be supplied to individuals
separately, so they can be financed individually, as is informal education by books, lectures, visits to museums, travel, and so on. They are
predominantly not *public* goods in the sense that they cannot be refused to people who refuse to pay; they provide separable private services. They may have beneficial external effects in the sense that we all
benefit from living with fellow-citizens who can read and write. That is
a case for encouraging people to buy education by giving them cash
(or vouchers) and possibly for setting school-leaving ages, but not
for universal government control and tax financing of 'free'
schools.

Education is not supplied to individuals, or families, and paid for by
prices (fees) instead of taxes because of the errors of intellectuals; the
lack of vision of politicians; the empire-building pressures of officials;
the resistance of teachers to change. And it is not sufficient for
politicians, officials or teachers to reply that, whether my argument is
right or not, we 'cannot turn back the clock', or we 'must start from
here'. These are little more than the alarmed reactions of people who
fear change, who are finding reasons for rationalising their prejudices,
who have probably never thought of better methods of financing, and
who are putting themselves before the public who pay them. There is
nothing impracticable in changing the financing of much or most of
education from taxes to prices. The one requirement is sufficient
public understanding of the issues, on which individual parents, who
ultimately pay the teachers, have never had a chance to give their opinion in a way effective enough to change policy. Once the change is
demanded, it could be introduced. The obstacles are man-made and
removable by public pressure.

The reigning error

The errors go back to 1870. For many decades, since the early 1800's and even earlier, education had been spreading without government organisation or collective payment by taxes. The first state subsidy to (*private*) education came in 1833. Even from what we should now regard as tiny incomes, parents were finding the few pennies a week to send children to 'voluntary' schools (as parents are now doing in low-income developing countries in Africa and Asia). The schools expanded from rather under half a million children in 1818, not long after the Napoleonic wars, to over one and a quarter million in 1834, and they could not all have been the children of the rich. Parents were helped to pay the fees by church and lay organisations.

Education developed in the nineteenth century much more than was generally thought until recently. We used to be taught that it was so meagre as barely to exist and was generally harsh and inhumane. Some teachers using out-of-date text books still teach this history. They taught (and some still teach) that it was not until the state stepped in by the famous 'Forster' Elementary Education Act of 1870 (so named after W. E. Forster, the Liberal Minister in charge of education under Gladstone) that education developed substantially and systematically. But in 1965 an economist turned historian, Professor E. G. West, in a book at first regarded as notorious but now seen as a classic, *Education and the State*,[116] questioned the conventional reading of history. By a pertinacious study of the documents, he found the evidence that stunned and angered some historians. The sources, he insisted, had not been studied or had been misread. This is a fascinating story in historical detective work, and the debate among the economic historians continues. In further writings, especially in *Education and the Industrial Revolution*,[117] Professor West persists with his findings.

Briefly, it seems that even by 1851 two out of three million working class children were receiving some kind of daily instruction. It was, of course, short and inadequate by our present-day standards – only four, five or six years, ending around the age of ten. But it was spreading, and by 1870 more children were at school for more years than earlier, and were increasingly leaving later. Moreover, this schooling was entirely voluntary and almost entirely paid for by fees. Even where there was assistance from other sources (private, church or state grants) parents provided most of the money. The old myths linger in school histories, in fiction and in politics, but Professor West's evidence stands.

British parents in the nineteenth century

Are we surprised? Commonsense and an elementary understanding of human nature should have made us doubt the view that it was not till Forster's Act created 'board schools' that 'a national system of education' (the supposed purpose of the 1870 Act) was developing. What seems to have happened was that too much attention was paid to the spectacular writings of the social novelists such as Dickens, Mrs Gaskell and Disraeli who, like journalists and newspapers down the ages and round the world, attract attention by reporting and dramatising the exceptional rather than the general: it may be true, but it is not typical, and it makes bad history. Dotheboys Hall was a fictional creation based on a visit to a Yorkshire school in a cold winter in the late 1830's. Dickens, aged twenty-five or twenty-six, went with a false name and wrote up the school in *Nicholas Nickleby* in 1838. (A school history text-book published in 1965 still cites Dotheboys Hall as evidence of conditions in British schools.) Another economist and historian, Professor Mark Blaug, has found that, at least until very recently, conventional British histories of education largely ignored the evidence on the spread of literacy in the nineteenth century before the coming of state education in 1870. Yet school attendance and literacy in 1850 in England, *almost wholly privately-financed*, exceeded that in the world as a whole a century later.[5]

This neglect of the historical evidence probably reflects a perhaps unconscious sympathy with the massive critique of nineteenth century industrialism taught for a century by historians from Arnold Toynbee in the 1880's, through influential social reformers like Sidney and Beatrice Webb and historians J. L. and Barbara Hammond, to such present-day historians as Professor E. J. Hobsbawm of Birkbeck College and E. P. Thompson. The neglect of the historical evidence on the spread of private education may be repaired more quickly as the long-held but erroneous view of the effects of industrialism on social conditions is also questioned by its critics, notably Dr. Max Hartwell of Oxford and other historians. (Dickens' 'pious fraud' at Dotheboys Hall and its aftermath are recounted by Professor West in *Education and the Industrial Revolution*.[117] Dr Hartwell and other historians write in *The Long Debate on Poverty*.[33] Readers who have unwittingly accepted the social novels of Charlotte Bronte, Charles Dickens, Benjamin Disraeli, Elizabeth Gaskell, Charles and Henry Kingsley, Charles Reade, Frances Trollope and other writers of fiction as social history will find these two books as exciting as detective stories.

But the neglect of the nineteenth century evidence on literacy and spreading education paid for mainly by parents has done its work. The myth remains, stubborn and hard to dislodge, that education did not evolve spontaneously in response to parents' concern to educate their children but had to wait until politicians took it into their heads to tax parents in order to supply it 'free'.

Again I ask: why should we be surprised that parents, even a hundred or more years ago, wanted to educate their children? The question is of more than historical interest. For it points to two questions that are central to policy on education in the 1970's. First, if our grandparents and great-grandparents were sufficiently concerned about education to sacrifice the fees from their small incomes, are not we as parents today likely to be even more concerned about the education of our children? Second, if we (or at least 95 per cent of us) do not show that concern to the extent of dipping into our pockets, what is stopping us?

British parents in the twentieth century

These are the two most important questions we can ask about education. They are far more fundamental even than the one that seems to dominate discussion on education: whether all children shall be compulsorily channelled into standardised comprehensive schooling. The two questions are more fundamental because, until they are understood and answered to the satisfaction of parents, it is futile to discuss a form of education which *assumes* that parents have accepted educationists, officials or politicians as the ultimate arbiters of their children's education.

The answer to the first question must be that parents in the twentieth century would be even more concerned about education than their forebears were in the nineteenth. They would therefore be even more prepared to dig into their pockets. And, since their real incomes are five to six times larger, their pockets are five or six times deeper, the fees they would have to dig out (or the premiums on insurance policies or instalments on credit schemes to stretch the fees out over longer periods) would be impressively large. *Moreover, they would probably in total be larger than the sums they pay for education through their taxes.* In other words, we should now, as individual families and as a country, be spending *more* on education than we do. And the gap reflects the wishes of parents that are thwarted by state education.

Parents who pay, moreover, would not only add resources beyond those that can be raised in taxes. They would also expect their money to be used more effectively by paying more attention to the way it was being spent by the schools. Asian parents from the backward rural districts of India visit their children's schools in Britain to monitor their progress because they paid fees at village schools and saw education as an investment. That is how paying stimulates parents' interest. And that is why non-paying in Britain has made some British parents uninterested in the education even of their own children.

A tax is a loss of income; a price is a disposal of income

Would parents really pay more in charges than in taxes? The reasoning again is based on common sense refined by economic observation, most recently confirmed by the increasing indifference to the 'social wage' (which even shrewd but wishful-thinking politicians like Mr Denis Healey used to think as recently as a year ago should reduce the pressure for inflationary wage settlements). There is a clear, rational and predictable distinction between the attitudes to paying taxes and to paying prices. A tax is felt as a forced extraction of resources; it is seen as a reduction of purchasing power; it conveys a sense of *loss*, once tolerated but increasingly resented. A price is seen as a voluntary act of using personal resources; it is seen as an exchange of purchasing power for a desired commodity or service; it conveys a sense of *gain*, since voluntary exchange is a game in which both sides win. (Unless both buyer and seller stand to gain from an act of sale, they will not take part.) The difference is that in a free exchange *both* sides are willing; in tax-payments normal tax-payers are unwilling because they see nothing in return.

This proposition on the difference between paying by taxes and charges may seem self-evident, even trite. When I argued it in 1965[102, 103] it seemed obvious, certainly not original. Yet it ran contrary to the assumption underlying British social policy since then, and the whole thinking behind the Welfare State which seemed to suppose that people would want to pay more in *taxes* so that everyone else could obtain social benefits – the source of the 'social wage' fallacy. Trite or not, it explains much that has gone wrong with social policy in Britain – with the whole of the Welfare State – and it is the key to how social services in particular and 'public' services in general will have to be financed in the future. For it shows that if we are forced to pay by taxes instead of by prices we shall have less – of education, or anything else – than we should like to have and are able and willing to pay for. Payment by taxes – the financial mechanism of state education and the Welfare State – prevents us from doing as much in welfare as we wish and can.

This is essentially the nub of truth in the views reached by Houghton and Crossman. Their diagnosis of the deficiency in finances was the same as here, though their solution was to graduate the social insurance contributions and offer larger *state* benefits to people who paid more. The outcome would then depend on whether people saw the contributions as taxes or prices. This truth also seemed to emerge from studies I had worked on with Ralph Harris at the Institute of Economic Affairs in 1963, 1965 and 1970 discussed in Chapter 10.[31] And it is also confirmed by Professor West's conclusion after ten years of research that by jumping on 'the galloping horse' of fee-paid education in 1870 the state did not urge it on but probably slowed it down.

Parents would pay more in school fees than they save in taxes

So much for the first fundamental question. If, then, parents would by now be spending more on education in fees than they are paying for it in taxes, the answer to the second question (Why are they not?) must be the very taxes they have to pay to enable the state to provide education 'free'. Although people prefer to pay by service-related prices rather than by unrelated taxes, they are naturally reluctant to 'pay double' for private services after being taxed to pay for the 'public' services. As a result, the total spending on education (or health care, etc) is kept down.

This is the answer to two pretexts for state education: that many people could not pay the fees, and that, even if they could, they would spend their money on less worthy purposes. The first is circular reasoning: it is the state that makes people unable to pay fees. With a reverse tax to top up the low incomes the money would go direct from the parent to the school rather than through Whitehall or the town hall. Moreover, the bureaucracy would not cream off its upkeep en route. Not least, the money would go further because schools paid by parents would be more efficient in using resources to satisfy them: the dissatisfied customers' choice of going to competing schools would keep them on their toes much more than Parent Teacher Associations, Parent Governors or other second-best substitutes.

The second pretext for state education – that parents who could pay fees would not – is also weak. No doubt some would not. But this again is circular reasoning. If parents in the twentieth century would neglect their children's education more than parents in the nineteenth, that must be because they have never had to give much thought to it while it was being supplied 'free' by the state. The part of their minds that would have developed a stronger desire to educate their children has atrophied by neglect. It may take time to nurse it back to vigour as the method of payment changes from taxes to fees. Parents who require legally compulsory school-leaving ages to keep their children at school will need less compulsion as, in time, they learn the value of paying for education.

If, moreover, it were thought that returned taxes would not be spent on education they could, of course, be earmarked by being put in the form of a coupon or voucher that could be used only to pay school fees. The principle is essentially the same as the luncheon voucher, a paternalistic device in earmarked purchasing power designed to ensure that employees eat a sustaining meal. The education voucher would be a half-way house to the eventual policy of leaving income with tax-payers to use for education (Appendix 1). It could gradually be replaced by lower taxes, perhaps over twenty years, as the readiness of parents to buy education was strengthened by increasing knowledge of its benefits. And, as a final safeguard, a school-leaving age could be used as a long-stop for the dwindling minority of parents tempted to waste their vouchers by withdrawing their children early. Parental irresponsibility is an undeserved and insulting reflection on the good sense of working-class parents. It is no objection to changing from taxing to pricing in financing education.

How the education voucher would work

How would the education voucher work in practice? Its value could be calculated as the average cost of each child at a state school, or the average obtained by dividing state expenditure by *all* children, which would give a slightly lower figure because about 5 per cent are in private schools. It would be about £300 a year for primary schools, £450 for secondary schools and £800 for sixth-forms; and 5 per cent less if it included all children. It is a form of purchasing power that can be used only for the named purpose and, just as a luncheon voucher can be used to buy lunch at a restaurant of the voucher-holder's choice, so the fundamental principle is that the education voucher would be used to pay for education at any school of the parent's choice.

So much is clear in principle. In practice how the voucher would work would vary with local circumstances. The only experiment in the world so far was for several years in a school district in California. Conditions in some respects were different from those in Britain but parents found a new interest in education by being able to choose between schools (and also between 'mini-schools' in some of them). Here in Britain we must wait to see whether Kent County Council or any other local government will introduce an experiment.

Yet the general outline is clear enough. The secret of the voucher – the source of new 'parent power' it would bring – is that it puts parents into the circulation of the money for education. It makes them the new source of finance for schools. As the system of state education developed, state schools looked to their local education authority for money, and it in turn looked to the central government. Parents have not come into the financial circulation at all. No headmaster or teacher thinks of being paid by parents; and no parent thinks he is paying his children's headmaster or teacher. The link between customer and supplier is completely broken. The voucher would restore the link by giving the parent purchasing power and thus change him (her) from a recipient of 'free' education to a customer who pays for it with money. A voucher book could be issued each year with three vouchers, one for each term. The parent would take it to the school, to pay for education for a term; the headmaster would send the voucher to the local education authority, which would give him money in return.

The whole outlook of the school would thus change. Instead of looking to local politicians and officials as the source of its money for salaries, books, materials and so on, it would look to parents. It would thus want to know more and become much more aware of their opinions and preferences. The headmasters and teachers would, of course, retain the authority they acquire from their experience in teaching. A parent would, of course, still be *guided* by them. But no longer *directed*. The ultimate decision would be in the hands of parents, who would look for information and advice wherever they wished. Schools would be inclined to give much more information to parents, to welcome them into the work of the school, and to consult them on the reactions of their children to the school's teaching.

Teachers would remain the technical experts, but the respect they would win from parents would come from the quality of their advice and teaching, not from their status as employees of the local monopoly education authority. And in time the chances are that they would find more satisfaction in teaching children whose parents had chosen their school than in teaching children who were virtually captive customers who were stopped by teachers, officials, zoning or other devices from going where they preferred.

Strengthening and equalising choices

The range of choice would, of course, depend on the nature of the area. There would be more choice in towns and cities than in the country. But that is not an argument against having any choice in the towns at all, unless there is a virtue in the argument of the misanthrope that nobody should have anything unless everbody can have it. If you prefer to live in the country you may have a choice of only one church, cinema, garage or grocer. That is not a reason for not living in the country. It is your choice. It is certainly not a reason for making everyone who lives in a town or city have a choice of one church (what a row that would cause!), or one cinema, or one garage, or one grocer, or for putting all churches, etc. under state control.

All sorts of variants of the voucher idea can be envisaged. It can be taxed so that it has effectively less value for the family with more income than the family with less income. It can be confined to state schools but better extended to private schools to increase competition by comparison between them. Families can be allowed to top it up so that it can be used at schools whose fees are more than the cost of state schooling (though some are less). Or it can be available only for private schools prepared to accept it and not require topping up. [66]

The voucher idea has spread fast in the last year or two, and is also being discussed in Australia. The objections to it are fairly predictable. Some teachers may feel it would disrupt schooling, Labour councillors that it would stop the onward march of comprehensivisation, some Liberals that they cannot see how it would work, and some Conservatives that parents cannot be expected to choose schools. All these objections are questionable. They prejudge the whole matter by all allowing apprehensions to replace evidence. If they have some validity the evidence would emerge only if the idea was tried out in practice. None of the objectors has much of a case against *experiments* to see how the voucher would work, so that their doubts and objections can be tested. They may be well-founded. But no one knows. What we do know is that keeping parents out of schools has failed to produce good education.

Whatever the objections in theory and the obstructions from politicians, bureaucrats or union officials in practice, the central significance of the voucher that is more important than all else is that it is a device – probably the only practical one under present circumstances – of giving ordinary people, not least the lower-paid working man and his wife, the same chance of having a say in education.as the middle-class man who can pay fees, or the more monied man who can move home to escape a bad state school in the hope of being near a better state school, or anyone of whatever social class and income who can make a fuss and get his way by sheer persistence, nuisance-making, or bullying. This, of course, is not a criticism of people who pay fees for private schools or who move homes to give their children a chance of better state education; on the contrary they should be praised for sacrificing other things for their children. Neither is it true that they are necessarily the more wealthy: it is a calumny on working-class parents to suppose they do not care about education, or would not care more if they had the opportunity. The essence of the voucher is that it would enable working-class parents to be able to make the choices of those with more money who now pay fees or move their homes. In this sense it is egalitarian. And, moreover, like charging in general, it is *educational*: it would in time *teach* parents how to choose schools. That is the retort to middle-class people in all parties who claim that parents cannot be trusted to choose. If nineteenth-century parents showed they cared about education it is unhistorical to suppose that twentieth-century parents do not, or would not if they could. The boot is on the other foot: it is those who talk like this who are perpetuating a system in which parents will never learn care or choice.

Elusive externalities of education

A third pretext for tax-paid state education is that it benefits society as well as individual families and children, that children 'belong' to society as well as to their parents: school should therefore be tax-paid whether parents and children wish it or not.

This is an elusive argument. As discussed earlier, virtually every activity has externalities, beneficial or harmful. But, although strenuous efforts have been made to measure them, they often end in the mist of guesswork. Education was said to be a good thing for society in the nineteenth century because it would reduce crime or other anti-social behaviour. The chain of cause and effect is not clear, but in any event no one can show with conviction *how much* crime was avoided for *how much* expenditure. That is the relevant calculation. It is not enough to say 'education will reduce crime'. That is much too vague. It is the reduction in crime *at the margin* that must be calculated, compared and equated, for resources can be used in many other ways that people may prefer. A reduction in crime, even if certain, can be bought at too high a price in hospitals, housing, or pensions. And the onus of evidence is on those who make the claim. In any event, some forms of education, especially where parents are virtually excluded, may stimulate disrespect for people and property (would parents tolerate arson?), and other activities, like church-going, may reduce it.

The externalities argument is used much too loosely to justify untold public expenditure on anything that takes the reformer's fancy or captures the passing fashion. We should ask for more evidence than vague assertions from enthusiasts who want tax-money for their bright ideas but who will not put in their own. We should be especially on our guard when the expenditure is on a large scale and irreversible not least because among the opportunity costs are the piecemeal expenditures that have to be foregone on small-scale or local experiments to discover possible improvements in existing practices and institutions.

Are politicians better than parents?

Not least, we may recall that the 'children belong to society' argument or the 'government should save children from their parents' argument, has been used by tyrants down the ages, and in our own day in Fascist and Communist countries, to mould society to suit themselves, not the long-term interests of the children or their parents. The Hitler Youth was a short-lived nightmare; its Communist counterparts are continuing present-day realities. If the choice in the control of children and education is to lie between parents and politicians, there can be little doubt which a civilised society will prefer. Parents may go wrong, but they can be guided and advised; politicians can do much good but also much evil, and when they go wrong they are usually out of control except by civil war. Payment by taxes gives parents little say: perhaps that is why politicians (and teachers' union officials) like it. And that is why parents should want to pay by prices.

The argument for paying fees rather than taxes applies to all forms of education. Fees for nursery schools to increase the number of nursery places were commended by several members of the 1966 Plowden Committee.[124] Primary and secondary schools could be paid for by fees facilitated or encouraged by tax refunds or rebates, or by vouchers. Further and higher (university) education fees could be facilitated by tax refunds and loans. So could fees for teacher training and adult education.

No parent can obtain better education by paying higher taxes

To replace (or, in the early stages, supplement) tax finance by prices we must contemplate a structure of school fees. Before we go further into it we should deal with two objections.

First, why pay fees when we already pay taxes? The reply is simply that taxes are not enough. If you as an individual parent want to pay more in taxes, no doubt the Inland Revenue or the local council will welcome voluntary contributions, but your child will not receive better education. And if you think income tax or rates (or any other tax) should be raised for everyone, you are free to persuade the millions of other taxpayers to pay more in taxes than they are asked, or to petition Parliament to raise taxes for everyone. You will not have an easy task. Nor will you be popular. Even if you succeeded, education would remain 'free', no one would know what it cost, and still the advantages of individual pricing – consumer authority – would be lost.

Second, is it wrong to have to pay for a service you must use by law? This odd argument has been used for decades for 'public' services other than education. Is it really true that anything made com-

pulsory by 'the community' (a euphemism for Parliament, representative or unrepresentative) should be paid for by 'the community', that
is, by taxes? 'The community' lays down a myriad of regulations for
people as individuals or in groups (families, firms, voluntary
associations, schools, etc.) to observe and pay for. It is compulsory for
industrial buildings to have safety precautions, for firms to calculate
PAYE deductions, for public houses to have separate lavatories for
men and women, for hotels to have fire escapes, for motorists to have
third party insurance. Does 'the community' therefore pay all these
costs? Or should we insist that because, say, motor insurance is compulsory, it must be supplied by government, even if the motorist
believes he could get higher cover or a lower premium from a private
company?

What is wrong is not to pay in prices for a compulsory service but
the very opposite: for *it is inefficient to pay in taxes for a service that
need not be supplied by government.* If education (of a specified kind
or amount) is considered desirable by general agreement of citizens,
government need go no further than to lay down standards – ex-
aminations, or other methods of checking on education imparted and
acquired, school-leaving ages, and so on. What is improper is to oblige
people to pay in taxes for compulsory service *unnecessarily* supplied
by government without choice: and that is true of most so-called
'public' services because they are not public goods.

Events will increasingly enforce attention to charging, but public
opinion has yet to make itself effective. When the Government in 1976
was urgently considering cuts in its expenditure, a proposal from the
Treasury for a £10 a year fee for state schools was quickly rejected as
'politically impossible', without anyone asking the people if they would
rather send their children to deteriorating schools. Thus are decisions
made by the pundits, not by the people.

– but he can by paying prices

Whatever the differences of opinion about its quality, many people
think that state education is short of resources and should have more.
Others argue that it wastes a lot and may have too much. My argument is that, if taxes are not yielding enough to reflect family
preferences, some other source of revenue must be found, and that the
only new source is fees – or preferably topping up a voucher, which
would be better than fees at least in the early stages because it would

give all parents of children in state schools the new dimension of choice for which they would be prepared to pay something (Appendix 1).

The other facile solution – less spending on defence – is question-begging. To argue that the community would gain by diverting expenditure from defence to education requires knowledge about the value of marginal expenditure on defence which educationists cannot usually claim. As explained above, the choice is not between 'defence' (bad) and 'education' (good) *as a whole* but between additional (marginal) expenditure on one switched to it from the other. The National Union of Teachers is not an authoritative (or disinterested) witness on that judgment.

Would not fees for state schools reverse the tendency of a century? turn back the clock? go back to the bad old days? No. It would be a resumption of the natural wish of parents to educate their children. If the alternative to deteriorating education is higher taxes that people do not want to pay, the only way out is individual pricing in one form or another. Fees or vouchers would continue a trend that a century of 'free' schooling has interrupted, but which would have continued if the politicians had encouraged it rather than denounced it as immoral.

This is the shock that will have to be absorbed if British education is not to deteriorate further. In the short run, for perhaps twenty years, revenue from fees allied to vouchers is the best way to avoid larger classes or ageing equipment and all the other symptoms of financial stringency and official rationing of resources. But I am also proposing that pricing be built into British education as a long-term principle, on the general grounds that financing education by pricing is superior.

Resources for education

The proposal is that education costs – from nursery school to further and higher education – should be covered by fees, most of which would be paid by the device of the voucher, with a small proportion (say 10 per cent) being 'topped up' by the parents. With primary school costs at £300 a year for each pupil, parents could pay £30 a year, to top up a £270 voucher. With secondary schools costs at £450 a year, parents would receive a £405 voucher, requiring £45 a year. Sixth form costs are around £800 a year – voucher £720, topping up £80. A family with one child of each type could have three vouchers worth £1,395, requiring them to add £155, a small price for the influence and choice in education that state school parents have never had. Low-income parents could have 95 per cent or 100 per cent vouchers.

Let us begin with nursery education, recommended 44 years ago in the dark days of 1933 by the Hadow Report and again 33 years ago in the famous Butler Education Act of 1944. By 1966, 33 years after the Hadow Report and 22 years after the 1944 Act, 'nothing effective' had been done, said a Note of Reservation to *Children and their Primary Schools*,[124] the 1967 Plowden Report of the Central Advisory Council for Education (England), which courageously recommended nursery fees. This Note was signed by a distinguished group of academic and public people: Lady Plowden (the Chairman – or Chairwoman – of the Council), Professor A. J. (now Sir Alfred) Ayer, the Oxford philosopher, Dr I. C. R. Byatt, Reader in Economics at the London School of Economics and later Under Secretary (Economics) at the Treasury, Professor D. V. Donnison, then Professor of Social Administration at the London School of Economics and later Chairman of the Supplementary Benefits Commission, Mr E. W. Hawkins, Director, Language Teaching Centre, University of York, Mr Tim Raison, MP, the former Conservative Shadow Minister for Local Government, Brigadier L. L. Thwaytes, Vice-Chairman, West Sussex County Council, and Dr Michael Young, a former Director of Labour (Party) Research, of *Which?* fame, later Chairman of the National Consumer Council (appointed by Mrs Shirley Williams in 1975). Their intelligent Note raises several fundamental issues in the financing of nursery education that also apply to education generally. It is examined here in detail to see how the assumptions behind it typify the kind of establishment thinking that any radical change will have to confront in education or anywhere else.

First, it said the reason why nothing much has been done by government since 1933 was 'Quite simply there have not been enough resources, in teachers or buildings'. This remark is characteristic of the confusion of thought on 'public' services in general that has for a century made them public disservices and thwarted public preferences. It is the central error in the thinking of the pundits who have advised government and misled the public into denying itself services it wanted and could have paid for. There could have been – and were – resources for teachers and buildings. The trouble has been that they were misrouted elsewhere. The tragedy was that the state could not gather them *by taxation*. Parents had increasingly adequate purchasing power for nursery places but only a tiny minority thought of paying fees. (Local authorities would not always license nursery schools.) The vast majority did nothing about nursery places not because they had no resources (at least for a contribution) but because they simply did not think, or know, that nursery places were something – like dancing lessons, or music training, or sports coaching – they could pay for.

Equality means waiting for the slowest

The essential error in this reasoning of the pundits is that in a democracy where government scrupulously reflects public wishes, the state has to wait until a decisive number of voters are prepared to pay for nursery places in taxes before *any* parent can have a nursery place. In democracy as it is operated in practice, parents have to wait until government thinks it is politically safe to compel *all* parents as tax-payers to pay for the nursery places wanted by *some*.

But in this system, in which consumers are represented by government, no individual parent can obtain a nursery place by paying more in taxes – however much he or she is prepared to sacrifice other expenditure regarded as less important for the family. This is the end result of the view that some services, like education, should be equally available to all. Right or wrong, it has consequences that have rarely been discussed in Britain. By transferring decisions from the parent to politicians it reduces the total amount of resources channelled to these services. Parents who would be the earliest to pay for nursery places do not pay by fees and are not required to spend anything in taxes until a large number of other parents are also demanding them. But others who would follow once they had been shown what could be done have no information to guide them; so they are less likely to demand a 'public' service, and meanwhile they too spend nothing in fees.

The myopia fallacy

The eight signatories of the Plowden Note of Reservation proposed, rather tentatively and timidly, 'a parental contribution' to the costs of nursery education. They argued that the contribution would be for the benefit of children whose parents could not pay it as well as of children whose parents could. Without it, nursery education could not be extended at all, and the children of parents who did not pay would be no better off. With the new fee there would be new nursery schools or classes that could be attended by children of poorer parents both in 'educational priority' areas and others. Charging the parents who were richer (and/or had smaller families) would thus help parents who were poorer (and/or had larger families).

This reasoning is, of course, correct; but there is another fundamental error in the thinking that has dominated British social policy. If we are never to do anything in education (or medical care or anything else) unless it can be provided *immediately* for all, whatever their income, size of family or other circumstances, we shall be prevented from developing policy in ways that would help the most unfavoured families *eventually*. The argument for equality as deployed by egalitarians sometimes seems to have no dimension of *time*. Not everything can be done at once for everybody everywhere. The signatories knew that nursery schools would develop spontaneously in some districts sooner and faster than in others, but they did not seem to understand that gradual piecemeal development can be an advantage, not a defect. It enables those that come later to benefit from the mistakes of those that came earlier. And if they came earlier because local parents' incomes were higher (or, often overlooked, because they preferred education to other spending out of middling or lower incomes, as farm and town labourers did in the nineteenth century) they could confer the benefits of that experience on the poorer or the more conservative who came later. This externality of the rich (or of the not rich but loving) parent is usually overlooked, especially by sociologists who have approached social policy from the poverty end and who have put equality before the long-term interests of the poor.

Through the voucher to equality

In any event, the poorest and largest families can be helped to pay by making them less poor by general cash grants or by earmarked nursery grants in the form of a voucher. The Plowden minority, instead, favoured remission of fees, and then, in fear that some poorer or larger families would be too proud to accept remission and so would deny their children nursery education, they admonished them to remember that many parents, including the poorest, accepted state support for university education. 'If in universities', they asked, 'why not in nursery schools?'

This obstacle of pride would disappear if parents received vouchers, or even an additional nursery-school component on the family allowance (which hardly any parent, however rich, rejects). All parents would then pay the charge without social differentiation, with no exemptions as a source of social divisiveness, with more dignity for the poorer, and with no lack of take-up. There would be the added advantage that poor parents would feel they were paying on an equal footing with all other parents, not receiving a free gift for which they should be grateful. It would, far more than remissions, give them not only an equal voice with all other parents but also a voice made effective by the power of exit – to withdraw their child to another nursery school if dissatisfied.

Affluence and externalities

In urging the charge, the Plowden minority said they recognised that 'in public services benefits and contributions to cost cannot, and should not, be precisely equated. Public services exist where one cannot, and should not, try to [equate them].' They went on to give two very revealing grounds for arguing that nursery education was, perhaps, not nowadays a public service. First, people would not pay taxes to provide it, for themselves or for others. Second, parents were (in 1966) 'more affluent [and] more interested in education.'

The first reason seems to suggest that people become more unwilling to pay taxes for public services at a time when they are becoming more affluent. That notion conflicts with the theory taught by the leaders of British social thought, from the Fabians in the 1880's through the Beveridge-Liberals to the paternalistic Butler-Conservatives. What becomes of the theory of the 'social wage' in state benefits in kind like education that people will, we have long been assured, readily pay for? The second reason destroys two of the ancillary arguments for making a service public: that people could not pay (primary poverty) or would not pay even when they could (secondary poverty). 'Today,' said the Plowden minority, *they are for the most part able and willing to contribute.*' (My italics.) That is the most profound sentence in the Note by these eight eminent academics and public people. If people can and will pay for a service there is no reason on grounds of poverty or irresponsibility for making it public and paying for it by taxes.

Fees for nursery education are practicable and could be economic.

They are paid voluntarily in Britain on a small scale and in varying degrees in Western countries and Communist countries (including Russia). In Britain they are opposed by out-of-date conservative Tories, Liberals and Fabians.

Other forms of education

If this reasoning – that people are increasingly able and willing to pay – applies to nursery education, why should it not apply to other forms of education? They are also short of resources, and it has evidently been found impossible to supply enough out of taxation. People resist higher taxes no less for primary, secondary, further, higher, adult, teacher training, recreational, physical training, or any other form of education. They simply do not like paying higher taxes. Perhaps once they may have resented higher taxes less for purposes they approved, such as retirement pensions, [103, 104] but there is no knowing that their taxes will go to these causes. Even national insurance contributions are not earmarked for stated benefits, and there is no assurance that hard-pressed governments will reserve incoming monies for intended destinations. But if they are able and willing to pay for nursery education they are willing, and could be made able, by vouchers and lower taxes for all and reverse taxes for some, to pay for other kinds of education.

There is no shortage of money in Britain for as good education as the people want. How much there is in total and where it would come from are discussed in Chapter 10. Paying for education by fees from parents is financially possible, even though most have never thought of doing it and 95 per cent have never done it.

By 1978 or 1980, the cost of educating a child in a state primary school may be around £350 a year, in a secondary school around £600 a year, and in the sixth form £1,000. These fees could be reached in 3, 5 or 7 years, beginning with a nominal amount in the first year, rising by annual increments, and assisted by vouchers, tax refunds or tax allowances, by transfers of expenditure from other goods and services, for people with little or no income by a reverse income tax, and by earning to pay for something really worthwhile for the first time. There would be no hardship or injustice. There would be no disruption if the change took place over a period. But the transition should not be unnecessarily long. It should be short enough to encourage every family to give education the thought it has never had in planning the household budget.

Charging for choice

The transition would be eased by making education a better product than it has been in the past and so 'worth paying for'. The most effective way would be to supply the ingredient that is missing in tax-paid (in contrast to fee-paid) education: choice, and the influence and authority that go with it. The transition to full fee-paying by all parents would be eased if the new dimension of choice were created and made effective by returning taxes in the physical form of a document empowering the parent to pay for education wherever he found it to his liking. This is the education voucher.

Further and other education

Table C in Chapter 3 indicates the other main forms of education provided by local government, and now financed by local rates and national taxes transferred to local government.

Higher (university) education is financed mainly (about 90 per cent) by central government through the University Grants Committee.

The special schools are essentially for handicapped children and young people, who are not necessarily poor. Whether they should continue to be paid for by taxes turns on the role assigned to the family. If a handicapped child is regarded as the responsibility of the family, the parents should pay if they can, or be enabled to pay if they cannot. If the child is regarded as a responsibility of society, its cost should be paid by taxes.

None of further education is compulsory, so there is not even that pretext for financing it by taxes. The same applies to other education services, and to school food.

University students pay on average 10 per cent of their fees, often with assistance from local government. These fees could be raised to cover costs with the assistance over five years of loans and vouchers. The independent University College of Buckingham is the first pioneer for centuries in fee-paid higher education.

Overseas students are no exception. If it is decided for political reasons that Britain benefits by educating them, whether they are rich or poor, and whether their government will pay or not, they could be given vouchers to pay fees. To decide the value of the voucher, the external benefit (to Britain) would have to be measured, a difficult task that might yield estimates varying from substantial amounts to nil. (Detriments would have to be assessed as well as benefits.) But the hard-pressed British taxpayer should require something more than vague assertions of intangible externalities to support large claims on tax revenue. For the opportunity costs in higher pensions for older people with little other income, or in more money for the police, or for under-five play groups, must be weighed in the balance.

5 Medical care: making the payment fit the case

Few of us under forty-five remember paying for medical care directly. Yet few health services are public goods, in the sense used in this book. Preventive measures benefit everyone in the area whether they pay or not, so charging is impracticable or uneconomic; but hospital treatment is private, family doctor services are essentially personal, most local authority services are separable and personal – health centres, midwifery, health visitors, home nursing, ambulance, family planning.

There are some 'catastrophic' risks (such as major surgery or crippling diseases) against which it is very costly to insure, and people may fatalistically prefer to run the risks rather than reduce their living standards by insuring against a rare disease or an accident that may never happen. It is possible for individuals or for society as a whole to pay too much to restore health after disasters.

This reasoning may sound harsh, but it is people who ignore the 'opportunity costs' – the enormous sacrifice in education, housing, or pensions or everyday consumption required for total health – who are (unwittingly) callous. People make better judgements as individuals than in the mass. No individual man (or woman) thinks health must be secured at *all* costs: he (or she) would otherwise never cross the road, or smoke, or swim, or fly, or eat without a food taster. It is only the National Health Service – a mass, make-believe, macro-artifact – that teaches the myth that the best health can be preserved or restored 'free' for all. In practice it does not do what it preaches: it has to ration kidney machines, for example, and so condemns some patients to death. (And it is a bit of a fraud as a supposedly comprehensive 'National' 'Health' Service. It is both too all-embracing, since it comprises private benefits as well as public goods, and not all-embracing enough, since it does not supply all the services required for good health – the right food and other requisites.)

In the real world there are unavoidable or accepted risks to health, and treating ill-health uses resources. The costs can mostly be covered by insurance, and people with low incomes can be enabled to insure by a reverse income tax or by having their premiums paid on a sliding scale by government, as has been done in Australia. Catastrophic risks can be collectively tax-paid, as war damage was from 1939 to 1945. Most Western industrialised countries have mixtures of social and private, compulsory and voluntary, insurance. The result is that they channel more resources per head to medical care than we in Britain, who for the most part (95 per cent) are allowed to pay only by taxation. In Europe, North America, Australasia $6\frac{1}{2}$ to 8 per cent of the Gross National Product goes to medical care; in Britain it is barely $5\frac{1}{2}$ per cent. The higher figure indicates the advantages of diversifying sources of finance. Perhaps even more important, it reflects the preferences of the people who pay. This is the reply to defenders of the British system, which relies mainly on one source, who say that resources, even if less in Britain, are used more efficiently than in other countries. The reply is that, whatever the relative efficiency of the British state system, which is debatable, it does not allow people to pay in the ways they prefer. It is imposed on the people by politicians, officials and 'experts' who claim they know better. They have not been able to escape from it because all the political parties have supported it.

That is why we in Britain – and only we in Britain among Western industrialised countries – have a 'National Health Service'. The reason asserted for making people pay by taxes is that it removes the price barrier, so that everyone can have the treatment he 'needs' without worrying about paying. This may be the reason that moved the early enthusiasts for the NHS, like Aneurin Bevan in 1946, but it is still being repeated by his followers today, thirty years later, when social conditions have changed beyond recognition so that many can pay, directly out of pocket or by insurance, and when, in any event, the methods of dealing with poverty have been transformed and it is no longer an insurmountable barrier to medical care.

Not a public good: instant equality

The real, main motive for replacing prices by taxes in 1946, and for persisting with taxes despite the social and economic changes of the intervening thirty years, has nothing to do with medical care as a public good. Nor is the motive basically the desire to deal with poverty: that idea appeals to compassionate enthusiasts, but at the bottom it is a politician's rationalisation. The motive may have a tenuous connection with irresponsibility – by replacing the supposedly callous parent or relative and the amateur patient by the informed and kindly state. It may use externalities as a supporting pretext, though there are other methods for dealing with social benefits of medical care than abolishing pricing. It claims to have something to do with economy by avoiding duplication in medical services or insurance financing, though the NHS bureaucracy burdens medical care with delays and piles up administrative costs. And the NHS monopoly has no internal generator of efficiency.

The central motive for maintaining state medicine in the face of economic change is rather the anxiety of impatient reformers who want to establish instant equality; they dislike the reverse income tax because they think paying for medical care is 'obscene', and they cannot wait for incomes to be equalised as social mobility spreads the opportunity to learn and to earn.

Rationing health care

What stands in the way of equality of access to medical care (or anything else) is inequality of income. This inequality produces unequal *demand* for medical care, and it is tempting to take the short cut of making income irrelevant and equalising the *supply* by announcing that it is available 'free' without limit to all comers. This is called abolishing 'rationing by the purse'. It has externalities: it makes politicians important and creates jobs for bureaucrats.

But it does not abolish rationing. Since there is no price to apportion supply between the various demands, there must be rationing by other means. In the National Health Service medical care is rationed above all by time. 'First come, first served' sounds fair but it favours the fleet of foot, the loud in voice. People and patients who are rich in time receive more or better medical care than those who are poor in time. The more individuals can wait and queue, the more attention or the better treatment they receive. So the work-evading worker or the self-centred housewife has better access to the National Health Service and gets more out of it than the conscientious worker or the self-less housewife. What sort of equality is that?

The other rationing devices, no less arbitrary, are influence (if you know your doctor or hospital official you are treated better than if you don't), literacy (the middle classes who speak the same language as the doctor do better than the working classes), cunning (those of any class who know how to 'work' the system do better than those who resignedly accept it), sex-attraction (which favours women), blackmail (of doctors who will not readily sign certificates), and other arbitrary influences like political status which ensures earlier treatment for Ministers than for the tax-payers they are supposed to serve.

The irony of rationing under the National Health Service, which its enthusiasts will not face, is that these differences are even more objectionable than differences in income, which at least to some degree reflect differences in value to the community. For differences in influence and bully-power are even more difficult to reduce or remove. Favouritism is more widespread in the National Health Service than we like to admit, as it is in other 'free' systems in Russia, Hungary, Poland and Bulgaria. The NHS has not abolished inequality: it has driven inequality underground and made it more difficult to correct.

The strongest argument against the NHS and its replacement of pricing by taxing is that it prevents us from channelling as much resources to medical care as we wish. Evidence from other countries seems to show that tax financing reduces the funds for salaries, equipment and buildings for health centres and hospitals. Americans and others who return to their countries with praise of the National Health Service speak of their experience with it in emergency. People in their countries are not told (because tourists do not stay long enough to find out) of the months or years waiting for 'cold' surgery or 'elective' (optional) treatments that may turn 'hot' and imperative in the waiting. There is almost no discussion in Britain of the central reason why doctors emigrate and patients wait, surgeons lament inadequate equipment, research languishes, casualty departments are closed, wards are short of nurses. The central reason is that, since people and patients do not pay directly by fees but indirectly by taxes, the decisions are made by the politicians, guided and advised by officials, who can impose their notions of the good and the bad. And the 'good' notion for thirty years has been that price stands in the way of equality of access and shall therefore be banned *even if the resources channelled to medical care are less than they otherwise would be.* That is the truth that no amount of repeated assertion that 'the National Health Service is the envy of the world' can suppress.

Paying by pricing (through insurance) can be restored. The choice is between the 'planned', tidy, tax-financed National Health Service with less resources and a priced system with more resources, organised and financed by diverse methods. The obstacles are not technical but political: if we showed we preferred better medical care for all to less medical care (endured in the name of equality but still unequal in practice, whatever the objective), the politicians and the officials would have to find the way. The essential is that the red herring of equality shall be recognised and abandoned. Here as elsewhere it has barred the way to better service for all.

More resources for medical care

The extent to which better medical care could be available for all is indicated by the additional resources that would be assembled if we could pay by prices (based on insurance). We should then be spending, in all, in my judgment, something of the order of $6\frac{1}{2}$ to $7\frac{1}{2}$ per cent of the GNP, as they do in Europe and Australasia (even more is spent in North America). If we take the mid-way point of 7 per cent, we should be spending £7,000 million on medical care, not the barely £5,500 million that is all the state can extract in taxes for the National Health Service – or more than 25 per cent as much. The additional £1,500 million could go on higher pay for doctors, nurses and non-medical staff, better equipment, more pain-killing or life-saving medicines and machines, more new buildings and, not least, in ridding the poorest and the less articulate of the queuing and the waiting, the subservience and the obsequiousness that go with the tax-financing of medical care.

The medical services that should remain financed wholly or largely by taxes are those that are public goods with inseparable private benefits. They are the environmental and preventive services, largely local, shown in Table C of Chapter 3. The remainder of medical care yields separable benefits that can in principle be paid for by pricing (charges for goods, fees for services). When the third or fourth crisis in NHS finances came in 1967, 17,000 family doctors had signed un-dated letters of resignation (as self-employed they do not strike). The British Medical Association appointed a panel of ten doctors and two independent laymen to draw up a new structure of financing medical care in the event of a breakdown in the NHS. The Chairman was Dr Ivor M. Jones, a general practitioner of outstanding ability, dialectical skill and negotiating power. The panel spent two years, 1968 and 1969, studying the weaknesses of tax-financing in Britain and the wider varieties of financing used in almost every other Western country, as well as the methods used in the Communist countries, to see what could be learned. (The Western countries were Australia, Austria, France, Germany, Iceland, Luxembourg, the Netherlands, Belgium, New Zealand, Norway, Sweden, Switzerland and the USA.) It reported in April 1970, but by then the government had granted terms the doctors considered acceptable, and the 600-page report, *Health Services Financing*, was pigeon-holed (and cold-shouldered) by the BMA hierarchs, perhaps because it had become an embarrassing reminder of earlier friction with a government with which the doctors had come to terms. But five years later, in 1975, the fifth or sixth crisis in the long history of chronic financial deficiency came when the swollen government spending made possible by three years of mounting overseas borrowing was cut back. This contraction, combined with the apparent determination of the Government to increase the tax-financing from 95 to 100 per cent and squeeze out private medicine, brought stronger action from the doctors than ever before, including unprecedented working to rule and strikes.

Hitherto the hope of doctors had been that they would be able to persuade a strong Minister, Labour or Conservative, to squeeze more for the NHS out of the Chancellor of the Exchequer in the Cabinet room. Sir Keith Joseph is said to have succeeded with Mr Anthony (now Lord) Barber in 1971 or 1972. Mrs Barbara Castle is also supposed to have had some success in 1974 and 1975. But since late 1975 cuts have been the order of the day, even for the 'essential' NHS. Some senior doctors then began to wonder whether the NHS would ever find as much money for medical care as they thought it should and could have. Apart from some flirting with the fond hope, which has long attracted doctors, that government would give them the money through a Health Corporation or some such mechanism and let them spend it as their medical judgement told them and without political intervention, they returned to the argument of the Ivor Jones report as indicating the alternative to tax-financing in their evidence to yet another Royal Commission in 1976.

Like the agreed unanimous reports of all committees, the Ivor Jones Report was a compromise, but it was the first attempt since the foundation of the NHS to document a new financing mechanism in place of almost total reliance on taxation. Because the doctors, some with reluctance, were at last prepared to contemplate a change from taxing to pricing, as one of the independents I signed the report although I did not agree with its proposed division of health services between tax-financed and price-financed (based on insurance). (There was a puzzling BMA prejudice in favour of 'free' drugs.) It would have clarified the argument if I had put my list in a minority Note. But the central principle was established, and worked out in some detail, that tax-financing was not suitable for all medical services.

The sole criterion for obligatory tax-financing is whether a service is a public good with inseparable private benefits. Other reasons – inequality in income, efficiency, monopoly, etc. – may make taxing desirable but have to be proved. On this principle, hospitals, general practitioners and dental and ophthalmic surgeons and local authorities can be paid by fees (which can mostly be insured). Drugs and appliances, too, could mostly be covered by insurance. It is true that half of the 450,000 hospital beds are occupied by long-term chronic cases of old and mental patients, who are not all poor but whom it may be administratively simplest to finance by taxes. Severe or 'catastrophic' acute cases, such as polio, or heart disease, or kidney failure or major accidents may require heavy expenses that are difficult to insure. These also may best be paid by taxes if they cannot be covered by state-assisted insurance.

Evolving a refined structure of charging

In all, a much more refined financing mechanism is required than taxation, both to minimise the deterrent effect to patients of fees or insurance costs and to use price as a reminder to them and to doctors and nurses that medical care uses scarce resources that could be applied elsewhere. Other countries such as Australia and the USA have gradually evolved and refined mixtures of voluntary and compulsory, state and private insurance, coinsurance or 'patient's fractions' (where the patient bears a proportion of charges shared with the insurer) and deductibles (where the patient bears the first slice of the charge), state assistance for low-income people to enable them to insure along with everyone else, and so on. These mixtures are not as tidy as tax-financing, which is what politicians and bureaucrats prefer, but for patients their very advantage is that they are all more varied and flexible, as they should be in financing the wide range of services, from emergency treatment for heart failure to optional surgery for varicose veins, that in Britain are bundled together and described, grandly but simplistically, as 'the National Health Service' – a name no scientist or patient or economist concerned with individual circumstances would have given it, but which comes naturally from an administrator or a planner excited by organising services for large numbers.

The main triumph of the mixed systems overseas is that they maximise the resources for medical care, which the NHS does not. More accurately, they approach nearer to the *optimum* amount, in the sense that they enable people to say how much they want to spend on medical care at the expense of all the other goods and services they could have. These mixed systems create no false hopes and no myths. They show what the vast range of medical services cost, and they allow people to pay in the ways they prefer. They have created no Nirvana, or mirage of 'the best medical care for everyone', which we in Britain have been misled into thinking was not only possible but what the NHS was giving us in our everyday lives, but which it has not given, does not give, and cannot ever give.

Here again the voucher could be used to ease the transition from taxation to charging. In medical care it would cover not fees, as in education, but insurance costs, or a proportion of them. Topping up the voucher out of pocket would be the source of additional finance for medical care. The IEA surveys again showed impressive interest in health vouchers in all social classes (Appendix 1). More than a third of the highest incomes and (even more surprising) more than a quarter of the lowest incomes said they would make up a two-thirds voucher if they could insure privately. These proportions would grow once the system started.

6 Homes: ending the rent-tie

A third of us (or more) have never paid for our homes – directly. For increasing millions, housing is another long-standing 'public service' that is not a public good. It can be supplied separately to individuals and therefore paid for directly by prices (rents, or mortgage repayments, or purchase money). Yet it remains paid by taxes, in part or large part for millions. In all, taxes have paid around 40 per cent of Council rents (Table C).

Indictment of house-financing by taxation

Restricting rents began in 1915 with the aim of limiting the rising costs of living in wartime. As a short-term measure it might have been convenient, but it has now lasted over sixty years. It has spread to 6 million households in government-owned homes and $4\frac{1}{2}$ million in private homes. It has dried up private investment in house-building to let. It has entangled local government in owning houses and building them, sometimes by costly direct labour. It has forced central government to provide large subsidies. It has brought rationing by official rules, favouritism by officialdom, personal frustrations, political bribery and bureaucratic bullying, the corruption of government officials and local government, the spilling over of rent controls to privately-owned homes. It has intensified immobility of labour penalised by losing rent subsidies if it moves house. It has created the vested interest of direct (building) labour. It has manufactured a large constituency of rent-favoured yet degraded tenants, and made politicians more concerned with how tenants will vote at the next election than with the efficient use of resources in home-building and maintenance. With the best of intentions rent restrictions have had the worst of results: in intensifying shortages of homes, worsening dilapidations of existing structures, destroying the incentives to build, and ignoring people's preferences. More perhaps than any other social policy, British housing displays the abject failure of political sensitivity to public circumstances and preferences that is the disagreeable reality behind the facade of 'public' service.

None of this was unavoidable. It has happened not because rent control was the only way to deal with rising rents or low incomes but because it was the politicians' easiest way to public favour by being seen to be protecting the poor in general and the tenant in particular against inflation or 'landlordism', the declamation of the demagogue down the decades. Politicians in all democratic countries display the same anxieties to be seen to be up and doing: rent restriction has been their favoured instrument in Europe, North America and Australasia. And always it has the same results.[25]

Political difficulty of removing tax-finance

Even when politicians come to see the results of tax-finance on housing, and are appalled, as they gradually are becoming in Britain, they encounter the same difficulties in ridding the country of the cause. Even when it is removed (as largely in Australia, though it lingered in New South Wales), the memory of it and the fear of it returning continue to deter the building of homes to let and so perpetuate its results long after it is discarded. Austria, the USA, France, Britain, and Sweden tell much the same story. In all of them (and some others) valiant, painful efforts have been made by a few brave or more sensitive spirits among the politicians to thaw out the ice of frozen rents, as in the British Rent Act of 1957 (for which one of the Conservative intellectuals, Enoch Powell, should be praised). The 1965 Act re-froze the ice by extending controls. The 1972 Housing Finance Act tried to rethaw the ice by replacing subsidised rents with rent allowances (cash) for private tenants and rent rebates for council tenants, but was obstructed by political demagoguery. The 1974 Housing, Rents and Subsidies Act, which froze the ice on rents for furnished flats, has dried up their supply.

Politicians in all parties who saw the case for thawing out rents have defended their inaction with the excuse that rents could not be raised to cover costs as long as there was a scarcity of housing. This is putting the cart before the horse. There is always a scarcity of housing, as there is of everything else, otherwise there would be no prices. Charging less than 'economic' (market) rents itself creates shortages by swelling demand and choking off supply. A rise in rents nearer to current housing costs was a necessary pre-condition for diminishing the scarcity and removing the shortage by increasing the number of homes built. The real obstacle to an increase in building for letting was the lack of faith that the politicians would raise official rents nearer to housing costs, or that, having raised them and abolished rent controls, they would not be tempted to restore them for electoral reasons.

Whenever an opponent of reform obstructs it by admonishing us to 'face the facts', to 'start from here' and begin with the undesirable policies and practices we wish to reform, we should reply that to reform the present we must understand not only how it began but also what could, or would, have happened in its place. There are still some Bourbons (in all parties and none – like Shelter) who have said that the fault with rent control is that it is not strict or extensive enough. They have had their way; in 1974 it was extended from unfurnished to furnished rooms; students who want furnished rooms are learning first hand of the difficulties of families who have long wanted unfurnished flats or houses but found they had vanished.

The long leap in restoring market prices

To the more intelligent but conservative-minded, and to the timid in all parties who say that rent restriction is unfortunate or dreadful but has come to stay, and all that can be done is to remove its worst effects by making rents a little more flexible, we must reply that if you are surrounded by a swamp a short step is futile: the only hope is a giant leap.

A long leap is now the only hope of escape from the bog of rent control. It will become possible when the people understand what would have happened if rent control had been nipped in the bud in 1919 after the First World War before it had sunk its roots, before it had frightened off people who would otherwise have continued the pre-1914 development of investment in home-building to let, so that in 1919 local government had to be required by the Housing and Town Planning Act to build the first of the Council houses that now house more than one family in three. The alternative that would have developed since 1919 is home-ownership. By now we should have had not the 50 per cent of households it recently reached in Britain (9 million home-owners out of 18 million households) but the 67 per cent as in the USA or 75 per cent as in Australia. Three to five million rent-paying tenants in Council or private houses or flats would be owner-occupiers. When the public understands that this is the perfectly practicable alternative, ways will be found by politicians and officials, and we shall hear less of 'difficulties' and 'facing facts'. When a politician 'faces the facts' of electoral opinion, voters' displeasure or ballot box rejection, he finds ways to act.

The only fundamental solution to the politicians' failure to stop the (partial) financing of housing by taxes is to replace them by prices, that is by rents. The only long-run solution to the evils created by lingering tolerance of restrictions on rents is to remove the restrictions. The only lasting solution is to let people pay for their homes by prices, by allowing rents to rise to the amounts agreed between suppliers of homes to let and people who want them. This is the only way of allowing people to decide whether they want to continue as tenants or to own their homes. Since in time more (perhaps most) tenants of rent-restricted Council or private homes would move to ownership, Councils could at last move out of owning and building homes into which they should never have been misled by central government, and private owners would put their rented houses and flats into good repair and build more for people who preferred hiring to owning their homes.

Here again the voucher could be used, initially to help low-income families and then rent-restricted tenants generally, both Council and private, to rent or buy homes of their choice. In Australia a Housing Assistance Voucher Experiment is enabling tenants in 'public' housing estates to escape to other areas and to private housing.

The argument that subsidies to purchasers of homes should be removed in parallel with subsidies to tenants raises wider issues. Removing the tax allowance on mortgage interest would logically require the removal of all fiscal encouragement to long-term saving, as in life assurance and pensions. To avoid biasing the choice between tenancy and ownership, all subsidies should be removed. If it were desired to encourage home ownership in all income groups, the objection to the (income) tax rebate on mortgage interest is that, by definition, it varies directly with income, so that the man with higher income who buys a larger house with a larger mortgage receives a larger subsidy than the man with lower income who buys a smaller house with a smaller mortgage. But that is a consequence of progressive taxation. If income taxation were more proportional, the objection would be weakened. If the tax assistance were varied indirectly with income, as it could be in a housing voucher, the objection would have changed its ground.

Second-best solutions

Raising rents to cover costs is the best long-term solution. All others are second-best. It is the measure of the long years of political neglect that second-best solutions should have to be sought. They all have the flavour of short-cuts – from selling Council houses to occupying tenants at a privileged price to ease them out, to giving Council houses away in order to get tenants off rate-payers' backs. They are best used as means of hastening the long-term solution. A package of policies, comprising the long-term solution and short- and medium-term cuts in tune with it could be:

1 All rents, Council and private, to rise by annual instalments to cover housing costs in four years;
2 between 1977 and 1980 local authorities to be empowered to offer tenants first claim on Council houses to be sold by auction[79] either (a) individually to occupier-buyers (existing tenants or others) or (b) in parcels to home-renovators for improvement and re-sale to individual occupier-buyers in the open market;
3 tenants under 45 with income below a stated sum to be offered matching finance of £1 for £1 found for the deposit on a home; half to be repaid in 7 years;
4 tenants of 45 and over with income below the stated sum to be given half of the deposit; a quarter to be repaid in 5 years; pensioners with no other income to be left in occupation for life, without succession;
5 from 1977 to 1980 rent subsidies to be made mobile to remove the penalty on mobility.[77]

Tenants would by these measures be enabled to make informed decisions on renting or owning, staying put or moving, and be given incentives to change to larger or smaller homes, and so on. Millions have never made these decisions, or have not made them for years, so that many are in the wrong homes and places, and are using methods of payment that no longer reflect their underlying preferences. In this way people would sort themselves out and end by living in homes that suited them better; they would no longer be tied to their houses or flats by outdated subsidies, they would make better use of the stock of homes, and they would have an effective mechanism (rent-price) for indicating what sort of homes they wanted.

In housing, as elsewhere, charging rather than taxing, when the results of both are explained, is what the people would prefer. It is not public opinion but political punditry that stands in the way.

7 From reading to rubbish

There could be no more decisive demonstration of the argument for changing to the maximum possible extent from taxing to pricing 'public' services than the talk-in between the political and bureaucratic pundits far over the heads of the populace on PESC, PAR, PEC, and PAC (below). The score in debating points has swung this way and that. The outcome is still in doubt. The pundits on both (or all) sides seem to be enjoying it. There is hardly a rate-payer or tax-payer in sight.

Here is Mr Roland Freeman (Conservative), formerly finance chairman (a sort of local Chancellor of the Exchequer) of the Inner London Education Authority (ILEA) and later of the Greater London Council (GLC), doing battle with Lord Diamond (Labour), former Chief Secretary of the Treasury. Lord Diamond had said that 'public' (my quotation marks) expenditure programmes had 'built-in driving power so that if they were not stopped they would consume nearly all, or all or more than all, the resources regarded as appropriate.' [20] Mr Freeman retorted with three ways that, he claimed, could yield 'a rich harvest of economies': abandoning instead of merely postponing capital projects in 'public' services, a ruthless pruning of programmes to slim down fat instead of 'the sporadic' forays of PAR, and, 'most revolutionary' of all, cutting the number of administrators which Lord Diamond had said could not be done. [22]

There was some reference to the restive taxpayer, but neither thought of letting *him* (or, perhaps more effectively, *her*) make the decisions of what, where and when to cut, which is impossible as long as they pay compulsorily by taxes. PESC, PAR, PEC and PAC are machinery and instruments devised, debated and deployed by the politicians and the pundits that the public pays for but has never (well, hardly ever) heard of. PESC is the Public Expenditure Survey Committee created in 1971 to produce five-year plans, which Cabinets hardly take seriously because decisions are usually made hastily, under pressure from interests not bothered by well-laid five-year plans, by Ministers more concerned with elections than with avoiding over-spending (which in any event, the Opposition may have to contend with two or three years later when their turn comes in Government). PAR is Programme Analysis and Review, created in 1970, that investigates suspected excessive expenditures but spasmodically and often too late. PEC is the (public) Expenditure Committee of MPs that examines estimates of 'public' (i.e. government) expenditure, in particular to see how the policies they imply can be carried out more economically; it has power to investigate but not to require government to heed it if Ministers think its recommendations politically inconvenient, as they usually have done. And PAC is the Public Accounts Committee of the House of Commons (15 members, Chairman usually from the Opposition), the main job of which is to see whether the money granted by Parliament has been overspent or misspent by the Department to which it was granted. If money has been overspent the PAC reports on whether there is objection to the shortfall being met by an Excess Vote. It investigates possible waste of public money brought to its attention by the Comptroller and Auditor General. A Treasury Minister is a member but hardly ever attends. (The public, whose money it investigates, is not allowed in.)

Much of this machinery has been ineffectual. It requires action by politicians. But Labour politicians, the Socialists among them rather than the Social Democrats, do not believe that government expenditure can ever be excessive. And Conservatives, with a handful of exceptions, would temperamentally rather avoid announcing 'cuts' in the hope that economic growth will make them unnecessary. PESC, PAR, PEC and PAC are macro-economic machines for dramatising and identifying 'cuts' that government will defer as long as it can. *What is wanted is micro-economic machinery that will enable each man and woman to make the cuts themselves in the privacy of their homes.* For that purpose they must know the savings they could make by cutting out marginal bits of services here and there after comparing them and discussing them with wives, husbands, children. The information they must have can be given only by telling them costs and charges.

Macro-ignorance and micro-knowledge

How many of us know the cost of a year in a nursery or secondary school? or in an evening institute or teacher training college? of borrowing a book for a fortnight? of a visit to an art gallery? a week of home nursing or a three-mile trip in an ambulance? a home help for a week? a meal on wheels? a visit from a police patrol to investigate a burglary? two fire-engines and crew to douse a chimney fire? a four-day court hearing to settle a neighbour's boundary dispute? removing 500 gallons of sewage? or half a ton of refuse? an hour at a swimming pool? the use of an allotment for a season? an hour's car-parking? the use of 50 miles of main road?

These and others you will recognise as the so-called 'rate-fund' services of local authorities that are supposed to be provided free (wholly or largely) out of the rates. Is it not arrogant of government to think it can cut intensely *personal* services without asking any of us what effects cuts of varying sizes would have in millions of our homes? And are we not likely to make cuts more readily if we make them ourselves so that we can minimise the inconvenience, discomfort or pain?

That is not all. Suppose some of us, or many of us, decide we should prefer to make no cuts at all, or only in the services we feel we could most easily sacrifice. Then we have several courses of possible action in maintaining the services we value highly. First, we could reduce expenditure on private consumption goods like everyday household purchases. Second, we could reduce new savings. Third, we could draw on existing savings. Fourth, and not least, we could try to earn more to keep up our expenditures on services we felt we would rather not sacrifice at all. None of these four 'feedback' reactions, which could yield large new funds for education (through fees), medical services (through insurance), roads (through tolls), etc., is likely if the government finds it can defer cuts no longer because of lack of revenue from taxes (or for home and overseas loans) and makes wide-sweeping 'cuts', in which none of us has any say at all as individuals. And this, of course is what has happened more than once recently in existing or projected nursery schooling, school, university and polytechnic building, hospitals, roads, police civilians, fire services, research and training, libraries, environmental services, etc. As usual, capital expenditure figured largely because it does not reduce services immediately and is therefore politically less unpopular for hard-pressed governments than cutting current expenditure. This kind of political motivation in the supply of public services may make them inherently inefficient. I am here assuming they continue to be supplied by government and discussing only the method of payment: by macro-taxes or micro-prices.

To make possible this better-informed decentralised structure of micro-decisions, we must therefore know relative costs and prices. We can then pay the charge if we prefer to go on receiving a service, which itself will cause us to think twice or encourage us to find ways of going without, or doing it – or part of it – ourselves, or finding cheaper suppliers, public or private.

'Do-it-yourself' cutting

A glance down Tables B and C will stimulate the reader to think how he and she and the family and household would react in several kinds of circumstance if people were allowed to react *separately*, micro-economically, according to individual, personal, family decisions instead of being part of a mass or a herd responding powerlessly to macro-economic decisions made by uninformed government. These circumstances are basically two. The *first* is a crisis period, such as since 1970, of over-spending by local and central government that has to end because the borrowing that bolsters it cannot go on till Kingdom come. The *second* is the more fundamental long run in which, at last, we elect a government to treat us like sensible people and recognise our ability to decide which goods and services we can largely judge and select for ourselves.

In the recent period of over-spending, by both Conservative and Labour governments, the two alternatives we have been proffered by politicians are higher taxes or deteriorating 'public' services. This is how the two Prime Ministers of 1976, Sir Harold Wilson and Mr James Callaghan, spoke. That is what the newspapers, with few exceptions, said. It is not true. There is a way to maintain the public (and social) services, or at least those that the people want to maintain, without continually raising taxes. It is to pay for them by charges. Payment by charges would also indirectly make them more efficient by encouraging competing suppliers outside government.

Consider the macro-economic action of the politician, and ponder its clumsiness. A circular from the Department of the Environment to local authorities in December 1975 offered 'advice' and 'guidance' on restraining expenditure to help the central government fight inflation. The general theme was that there could be no improvements in public services and that new commitments made unavoidable by changes in birth-rates, etc. must be compensated for by reductions in services or by economies elsewhere. In April 1976 the government White Paper on Government Expenditure repeated that 'any increases in individual services, whether for demographic or other reasons, must be offset by levels of provision in other services.' It then listed reductions in government expenditure on housing, environmental services, police and firemen, education and libraries, and social services for several years to 1980. It made them seem mostly tolerable pauses on a road of steady progress onward and upward. But let us examine three examples: pre-school facilities for the under-fives, libraries and water.

Penalising the pre-school child

A member of the Merseyside County Council and of the Association of Metropolitan Authorities Social Services Committee, although trying to put the best face on things, was moved to say:

> the public expenditure cuts are painful . . . At first sight, the cuts . . . in nursery education for the pre-school child in particular . . . are horrific . . . a virtual standstill on all new work . . . a far cry from our cherished dream of making top quality provision available for all children in these vital years of their lives . . . the backlog of shabby schools still in use . . . no solace either from day care centres [where] the cuts will mean capital expenditure must be halted . . . places available hardly measure up to waiting lists for priority cases, let alone contribute to general demand from such as working mothers.[110]

There followed a learned argument in favour of some services against others, which meant little more than that social workers were caught up in fashions that might not last but (for reasons that might be abandoned before long) created pressure for government to spend here rather than there.

Fewer books for 'public' libraries

There was also a shock in store for libraries.

> . . . libraries are being forced to reduce services to a level that may do permanent damage . . . [They] are having to cope with budget cuts of between 15 and 30 per cent at a time when they need an *increase* of more than 15 per cent just to cope with inflation, or 40 per cent to meet the average rise in the price of books over a year ago . . . Buckinghamshire over the past year has spent only

£65,000 compared with £291,000 the year before. [Sunday newspaper]

As a result of the cuts, libraries were buying fewer books and appealing for gifts, or cutting hours by closing on Saturday afternoon, the busy session; the waiting time for 'popular' books is sometimes two years; choice, especially in fiction, is severely restricted; publishers were becoming reluctant to publish new fiction writers. A Library Association spokesman warned the government: 'we are not prepared to see library budgets cut by up to 30 per cent when other services are cut by only 10 per cent.' The implied threat – writing to rule? down pens? – was not elaborated.

A Society of Authors spokesman weighed in with: 'The local library is the most used neighbourhood amenity. Each year our libraries make 600,000,000 lendings. To cut back on this is a bad policy both culturally and economically.'

Moreover the (Labour) Government could be breaking the law (passed incidentally by its own party as recently as 1964): the Libraries and Museums Act makes it a duty of public libraries to provide a comprehensive and efficient service, which the Department of Education has defined as 1,000 books for 4,000 residents. Buckingham (500,000 readers) will be spending only a quarter of its required quota, Surrey only a half. Other counties are evidently also facing cultural deprivation, in the fashionable sociological jargon.

Water, water, everywhere short

There was an even more scarifying story about water. Britain has periodic droughts; quite rightly equipment is not geared to deal with the exceptional season but with the normal. So periodically the natural scientist suggests *technical* solutions. Desalination of sea water has been a spectacular favourite; a national water 'grid' has had its champions.

Meanwhile in 1976 Wales might have to cut off supplies to industry, said a serious newspaper, London might have to ban 'even garden hoses', and in Wessex a water official tried praying on a Botswana rainmaker's mat. The typically technical solution of the eventual water 'grid', begun in 1974 by creating ten water authorities for England and Wales, was bravely carting water from surplus to drought areas (an expensive business, as the brewers discovered a century ago when they established local breweries).

When the dry summer of 1975 was followed by the dry winter of 1975-6 and the parched summer of 1976, farmers were apprehensive of water rationing, which could mean meagre salad, vegetable and hay crops. The Wessex water authority bought four 4,000-gallon beer tankers, had 1,000 standpipes ready for rationing, and was spending £1 million to take water from rivers and cart it around the region. Garden hoses were banned in some areas; new boreholes were sunk. There was urgent talk of importing water – and perhaps paying for it with North Sea oil.

The cause of the troubles

These three examples of public services supplied 'free' illustrate the central issues. Pre-school nurseries for the under-fives reflect the common view of social workers that parents are incompetent, require guidance, or should have somewhere to deposit their young children while at work. Libraries were established over a century ago to provide the working masses with easy access to literature. Water was supplied free when English towns developed.

None of these three is a public good with inseparable private benefits. Charges would yield income to increase facilities for the under-fives, or prevent the run-down of libraries, or make people think twice about using and wasting water. In all three cases, none of the discussion seemed to acknowledge that there was any other solution than transferring public expenditure from other services (which the claimant was not competent to judge), or presumably raising taxes even higher. Paying by price was simply in no one's mind – the social workers', the librarians', the authors', the water engineers', the administrators'.

But observe the essential differences between paying by taxes and by prices. In the first, no one may have under-five facilities, all must have deteriorating library services, all must suffer the consequences of drought unless we *all* agree *collectively* to pay more in taxes (or, in practice, unless politicians, who control the means of payment and make the decisions, judge that we all – or a majority, or a muscular minority – agree). This method permits the most conservative-minded and the most stick-in-the-mud authority to stultify the most adventurous individual or firm, anxious to discover new ways to improve on old methods. In contrast, paying by price not only enables the uncommon, unconventional, inventive individual to propose new methods and solutions; it also taps resources that are not reachable by taxes where no-one may move unless everyone moves, or can be compelled to pay.

We have examined the basic services of education, health and housing. Suppose we re-examine every other 'public' service organised by government and financed by taxes (wholly or largely) and ask: 'Why should this service be run by government? Why should it be paid by taxes? Was there ever good reason? If so, is it still applicable? Has social or economic change made it inapplicable? Are there other ways of paying for it? Are they better?'

Let us now, then, re-examine afresh the wide range of services that we have come to regard as the natural function of government, national, regional or local, and see how many can be better paid for, wholly or largely, by price (charges, fees, etc.). As an introduction let us briefly recapitulate the origin, nature and functions of price.

Real and artificial prices

Prices are the rates at which goods and services exchange for one another. We are not confined to barter (as in schoolboy 'swapping' or bilateral deals of goods between countries). We use money (which is anything that is generally accepted in exchange for objects or services) so that we do not have to take what the buyer of our goods has to offer but can take money and use it to pay for something else he does not have but which we prefer. Prices are thus usually expressed in the form of money. As such they create crucial information that enables us all to know what the goods or services we have to offer will bring in exchange for all other goods and services, so that by comparing prices we can finally make the exchange that bring us the goods and services that give us most satisfaction.

Without this information we should be plunging about (almost) blind. Look what happens in capitalist firms or communist countries with no spontaneous pricing. Firms that have no internal prices try to reconstruct them by creating 'transfer' prices for raw materials or half-finished goods passing between departments (as in Unilever and Shell in Britain) or, in the last resort, 'hive off' departments to work as separate firms which then buy and sell among themselves (like General Motors in the USA). Communist countries with no internal prices that reflect the real underlying value of goods and services passing from industry to industry or plant to plant have tried two substitutes. They have used prices in the outside capitalist world as broad guides to the value of agricultural products, raw materials or manufactured goods. And internally they have tried to restore the advantages of pricing by ordering their plant managers to produce up to the point at which the cost of the last unit ('marginal cost') equals the price. Here in Britain we have similar problems of knowing how much to produce of tax-financed goods and services supplied without price ('free') or with a subsidised price lower than what would emerge as the market price. ('Need', whatever that means, is not much of a guide, because when something is available free 'need' can expand inordinately, almost without limit.)

Price that emerges spontaneously from voluntary exchange is not perfect. It may be impaired by lack of knowledge, distorted by monopoly on one side or the other, imperfect because of externalities. But there is no purpose in contrasting imperfect price in the real world with perfect price in a non-existent world. The only choice we have is between imperfect spontaneous price in voluntary exchange in the real world and its only alternative in the real world. The only alternative is price fixed by government, and the verdict of reason and history is that it is even more imperfect, or no price at all, which is even worse.

Prices laid down by government may or may not reflect real, underlying, spontaneous values. Ideally government can be thought to have access to all the information – political, environmental, etc. as well as commercial – and this should enable it to take into account the externalities in deciding where resources are to be used. Whether government that on paper *can* adopt this wider, long-term, disinterested and entirely public-spirited approach *will* do so in practice in the political world of short-term electoral and day-to-day pressures is widely *assumed*, without any reasoning or evidence at all, by people temperamentally favourable to government action.

The main defect of voluntary exchange pricing is usually said to be that it is paid out of earnings or wealth, so that people with more can pay for more, and people with little or none may have to go without unless they are helped. Until unequal earnings are seen as the reward of unequal merit, unequal access to services will be regarded as unjust. And it is true that, like an indirect tax on a purchase, price is regressive: it takes a larger slice out of a smaller income.

But this view, especially common among people concerned about social and welfare services, confuses price as emerging from the interplay of supply and demand with inadequacy of demand. *The solution is not to abolish price but to ensure adequacy of demand.* For, as was argued in Chapter 2, price also has unique characteristics. It is not a barrier, but a link. It is *desirable* as a measure of strength of desire, even though imperfect. It is *superior* as a method of rationing to other methods because it is more easily corrected for inequality. It is a more *humane* way of conducting human affairs than authoritarian commands or military force. It is *unique* as a source of information. It is therefore a *teacher* of care, forethought, husbandry. And it is *irrepressible* even if driven underground.

How far, then, must the existing 'public' services be financed by taxes and how far can they be financed by prices? Let us go through the familiar services and begin with what many people would regard as an extreme example: the police.

Police: public goods and private services

Protection against law-breakers, like burglars, is the job of the tax-paid police. But it does not follow that all their services must be paid for by taxes. Some of them, like general patrols by police-car or policemen on foot, are public goods (or, where they are corrupt, public bads). Others, like advice on theft prevention, carrying money, storing valuables, convoying heavy loads, maintaining order at sports or social events, and others are separable personal or private services for which the police are or could be paid by fees. The county police forces have probably been understaffed for many years (although it is difficult to tell without pricing); and if tax revenue does not suffice to finance public order and safety it would be no more than good sense to draw on new sources of money to maintain and improve them. But it may be more than that: it may be essential.

> Wherever you live, if you took a short stroll from your home and were attacked, what chance would there be that your call of 'Police, police!' would be answered? In most cases none at all.

This is the view of Henry Cecil, the author and a County Court judge for 28 years (*Daily Telegraph Magazine*, April 1976). But that may be what people want if they prefer sports palaces or municipal theatres for their money (rates and taxes). If they want better police his solution is not original or helpful:

> Why then at a time of rising crime are there not enough policemen? ... because Parliament, while allocating funds for all sorts of frills, will not provide the pay to make a policeman's career attractive to recruits.

But a County Court judge is no judge of the competing claims on tax revenue of more policemen or of 'frills', which politicians may think more important for the welfare or happiness of the people, or for their own popularity. If it is desired to prevent or detect lawlessness, the task that requires solution is that of raising more money for the police. No individual taxes are earmarked for individual 'police funds', and people in general will not readily pay taxes for better police service from which they personally (or as families or households) may not benefit. Those who think they run little risk of burglary or other crimes will not see why they should pay for police to protect others whose risks are higher. But many people would pay more if they saw a direct personal benefit. That is precisely why there has been the development of 'private police' like Securicor, Group 4, and others to supply the *private* benefits of police protection.

The truth that Crossman saw in Welfare Services – that individual payment was not linked with individual services – applies to the police and everything else, even if conventionally regarded as 'public' services.

The important question is whether the police are providing, or are especially equipped to provide, direct personal benefits for which they could make charges to supplement the inadequate funds they are allotted out of taxation. They could then have more income out of which to raise pay, improve equipment and make their services generally more efficient. The assumption is that more funds will be spent efficiently, which they would tend to be if there were competition from private suppliers of personal police services.

General police patrols seem in principle to be a typical public good from which all in the patrol area benefit, from which they cannot be excluded, and for which they cannot be charged. But patrols benefit homes or buildings not according to their size (roughly reflected in their rates) but according to the value of the property (and life) protected. These values are reflected more accurately by insurance cover.[16] Police charges could therefore be made to reflect the varying value of patrol services to individuals or firms in the area according to the lives or property at risk. Whether the services responded efficiently to varying demands would remain to be seen. It may be that competition from private police services would be desirable as a stimulant and a basis for comparison as well as to supply additional services the public would not want from the public service.

The scope for charging is much larger. The police render, or could render, a wider range of services than is commonly supposed. In a quixotic reversal of political roles, a Labour MP Mr. Arthur Lewis proposed in 1971 (through a parliamentary question) that if the police charged for security services the shortage of manpower could be reduced. The Conservative Home Office spokesman replied that the Government did not think the police should 'go into business'. In spite of this obscurantist cavalier-Tory reply, the real public interest in a strong and efficient police force should override fusty notions about the impropriety of police 'going into business'.

The decisive considerations are the citizens' *demand* for security and other police services (in the economic sense: the amount they will pay for) and the ability of the police to *supply* them. And here the police are clearly equipped to offer services – convoying, guarding, advice, etc. – for which individuals or firms will pay. Chief constables are empowered by law to provide services at sporting events for fees, but in practice they raise a tiny fraction of police income from such services. This lack of development may itself reflect the shortage of policemen, in which event there is a vicious circle that can be broken only by Chief Constables becoming more entrepreneurial and making their services widely available and generally known. But that is difficult to envisage as long as they think they can fall back on taxes, which many must now begin to doubt.

No merit in public non-service

The police are schooled to think of themselves as public servants, 'giving', not selling, their services. This feeling may give them the sense of satisfaction in providing a 'public' service rather than engaging in sordid commercial selling. And this satisfaction is evidently common among government officials, teachers, social workers, doctors (or is it that they would rather not be paid directly – and judged – by their customers?). But if the obverse of this coin is chronic deficiency of equipment and manpower because of dependence on tax finance, the satisfaction must be tempered by the ironic *failure* to give the public the service it wants. A service that is 'free' but not available (or inferior) is nothing to boast about because it is not serving the public. Public employees who are *not* supplying debatably public goods – university and school teachers, doctors, nurses, and many others who are suffering from the shortage of public (tax) funds – must feel even less satisfaction when they reflect that people would be prepared to pay for their services personally rather than go without. 'Public servants' can hardly enjoy the prestige of their role if the method by which they are financed prevents them from serving the public when and where it wants them.

There may also be the reluctance of Chief Constables to draw income from fees for services unless a breach of the public peace is probable. This is the traditional view of the quintessential police function, which is another pure public good. But there is an awkward consequence for upholders of this view. If using police to attend demonstrations or marches of political extremists, student sit-ins, public protest meetings and strike picketing reduces manpower for other services and increases the danger to individuals from personal after-dark muggings, burglaries or trespassing, people will want to spend more on personal and private protection for themselves, their families and their homes, shops, offices, factories or other possessions where they feel they may derive direct visible benefit. They will spend more (privately) on safes, door locks, double glazing, alarm systems, stout walking sticks (perhaps fitted with weapons), guard dogs, private security services; and they will spend more on insurance as the long-stop if these measures fail to prevent loss, injury or damage. The public is thus forced into additional private expenditure because the public service for which they have paid taxes is not serving them efficiently, *because* it is paid for in taxes. Politicians who make policy on the police, and Chief Constables who execute it, will see that these measures in private protection are a consequence of the police concentration on collective protection – 'public peace'.

The policeman's dilemma

The police, therefore, have no monopoly of protective or security services, and will not have a monopoly unless government, to protect the public service, suppresses or excludes private effort by individuals to protect themselves, as it has done in education or medical care. This is the dilemma the police cannot ignore. If the police indulge a superior opposition to charging, they must not be surprised to see more development of private security services. Individuals exposed to personal or private risks will hardly listen to admonitions that protection and security are the functions of the public police forces. And, once they look to private services, the role of the public police will be further invaded, and there will be diminishing scope to develop the services of guarding, convoying, advice, etc., in which they could successfully compete with private services. The police must therefore compete with private services or face further contraction.

The police forces may thus have to develop services for which they could charge fees. 'Charging' the criminal may seem even more bizarre than charging by the crime-preventer. But there is no more case for free board and lodging in prison or detention centre than in hospital or school. And, as elsewhere, by restoring the awareness of cost, it would deter some lawbreakers by inducing them to 'think twice'. Larger fines for more offences and charges for detention would provide a fund for compensating victims. Fines could also be an alternative to detention, thus reducing government expenditure on over-crowded prisons, detention centres, etc., as well as increasing its income.

Personal fire services

This general reasoning – that public services that yield separable private benefits face a financing dilemma because they cannot escape private competition – applies to other services. Fire services are largely neglected as a source of income from charging. As with the police, charging seems to suggest a return to seventeenth and eighteenth century conditions when individuals made arrangements with suppliers to protect specified individuals or buildings. Some fire services, like general police patrolling, are public goods. Like diseases, fires can be contagious; people who do not pay for fire brigades in the hope of enjoying 'free rides' (or free fire-dousing) would thus be paid for by others who feared their neighbours' fires would spread.

But other fire services in the twentieth century are not public goods. Private security patrols protect life and property against fire as well as against injury, theft or damage. Evidently the demand for protection and security against fire is also, like that for police services, not being met, in quantity or quality, or both, by the public service.

Again the economic truth is that tax-financed fire services are not monopolies but are in competition with private services. Charging for existing services according to the service rendered to individuals, at home or at work, and extending services for which charges could be made, would seem to be desirable developments, although the charges would be crude until there were competitors for comparison. The alternative is to concede fatalistically that public fire services are unavoidably inefficient and try to forbid or prevent individuals from spending privately to protect their homes, cars, or places of work from fire. That would, no doubt, be resented even more by the populace than preventing or outlawing private expenditures on measures against personal injury, theft or damage, or on education or medical care.

Charges could be not only a reinforcement of tax revenue but a more accurate method of relating payment to prospective benefit. Fire services are financed in part by rates, which vary broadly with the size of home ('hereditament'), and partly by general taxes, which are broadly proportional to income. But neither rates nor taxes are a close measure of fire risks.[15] Here again a better measure could be the values (of buildings, possessions and possibly lives) covered by insurance. Thatched houses would thus pay more than tiled, and wooden factories than brick.

The advantage of paying the contribution to the upkeep of fire brigades in a charge rather than a general tax (rate) is that it would reduce the calls on the fire services because the charge would be varied to allow for fire precautions taken by each home occupier, shopowner, etc. Like price generally, it would act as a deterrent to avoidable demand. Rates and taxes unconnected with the degree of precaution taken by individual ratepayers have no such 'feed-back' effect on efficiency and cost.

Fire brigades could therefore be financed partly by rates and taxes to reflect the variation in individual risk and benefit. They could then have not only the prospect of more revenue from new private suppliers, but also, if they remain under-financed, more competition to fill the deficiency. Unless private self-help is outlawed, which is hardly credible, the police (and the doctors') dilemma re-appears.

Refuse collection

Refuse collection also has an element of public good in removing the externalities of noxious smell or nuisance, or risk of disease but it is separable and chargeable.[109] It is financed by charges in several countries. Street refuse is a public bad and its collection and disposal a public good. The earliest public scavengers seem to have been employed by the City of London in the early fourteenth century. The growth of towns in the first half of the nineteenth century strengthened the argument that removal of refuse would improve sanitation and health.

Politics rears its head even in rubbish. Industrial waste is charged for, though its collection is partly a public good; but it is politically safe to do so because the ultimate incidence of the charge (on consumers, suppliers, shareholders, workers) is difficult to trace. Yet the collection of home refuse is also both a private as well as a public good. Public nuisance laws may suffice to induce individuals to burn or remove refuse to avoid legal penalty. If those who hope for a 'free ride' allow refuse to accumulate, it may pay their neighbours to have it removed to avoid the spread of dirt and disease. This is the best case for refuse collection to be paid by taxation, but it is not strong. Social and technical change can alter public goods. It can hardly be argued that most people in Britain today would risk the health of their families – or even of their neighbours – by failing to remove rotting refuse. Domestic refuse collection is largely a separable private benefit that can be financed by charging. Its advantages are again those of price rather than tax; paying a charge varying with the quantity of refuse would encourage householders to sort refuse into the combustible, the re-usable and the disposable. Domestic or garden fires could burn the rest; glass, metal and paper would be saved for recycling; and the labour and resources (vehicles, land) used in disposing of useless refuse would be reduced. The advantages seem clear.

Refuse collection from homes in some countries on the Continent is paid for by charges. In the USA financing methods vary from municipal 'free' (tax-paid) collection to individual charges paid to private refuse-collectors at the extremes, with a lump sum paid by the local government to a private contractor in between. A recent survey of 2,000 cities covering a quarter of the population (210 million) found[101] that on average local government costs for a twice-a-week curbside collection were 69 per cent higher than those of private firms on contract. 61 per cent of the population were served by municipal collection (mainly in the larger cities); 63 per cent of the cities (mostly the smaller) have only private collection.

The 'information' function of pricing is illustrated by the comparison of collection costs in cities of varying size and for municipal and private collectors. In a city with 60,000 people, the cost of weekly municipal collection was 22 per cent higher than private contract for curbside collection and 35 per cent higher for back garden collection. The cost per household fell markedly with size of city up to 30,000 population and more gradually for cities up to 50,000, beyond which (and up to 700,000) costs were more or less unchanged. This information could be used by smaller cities (if there were an inherent inducement to economy) to reduce costs by joining together for refuse collection (municipal or private contract) and by larger cities to divide themselves into districts of about 50,000 and change from municipal to private collection. Individual charging was more costly than payment by lump sum on contract largely because of individual 'billing', but the survey did not investigate the effects of refuse-sorting by householders on the amount or value of refuse collected. Two hints of these effects were that 51 per cent of cities with municipal service had at least twice-weekly collections, about double the 26 per cent of cities with other systems; and in cities with municipal collections they were twice-weekly in 51 per cent where households have no choice but only in 33 per cent where they have. Competitive refuse-collection and charging thus seemed to reduce waste and increase efficiency.

Mounting refuse is a mark of industrial development and the rising living standards it brings in goods packaged for hygiene, durability and ease of handling. Some private companies offer inducements to their customers to return containers, such as empty bottles, but inducements are rarely offered by local government to retain, clean and return used materials. That is a small symptom of the big difference between competition and monopoly. Periodic generalised macro-appeals or exhortations from Ministers are not as effective as the direct, personal micro-inducements of pricing, whether as payment for 'empties' or charges for unloading unsorted rubbish. Here as elsewhere the tax-financed service is crude and insensitive. Charges could raise revenue for improved services and reduce the avoidable refuse that need not be collected by municipalities and dumped into expensive or unsightly tips. And it would induce efficiency by stimulating comparison by competition. Here again Britain is behind other countries in North America and Europe.

8 From roads to deckchairs

Charging for roads could help to improve the use of existing roads, gather more revenue for better roads, and even ultimately reduce costs by threatening competition from private toll-roads. Motorists can pay indirectly by road licence duty, petrol tax and purchase taxes on vehicles and accessories and valued-added tax on services, but these payments are only crudely related to the use of roads by individual motorists, so there is no incentive to think twice by road-users, or to provide the roads they would pay for. A motorist on a 'free' road is less thoughtful of the mounting costs than a taxi passenger with a meter staring at him and ominously clicking every quarter-mile. Nor has the motorist any idea of the cost of roads per Mini-mile (or Rolls-mile) even though he is sending up the tax bill against himself. And no individual motorist can make known his personal objection to un-satisfactory roads by withdrawing his custom. Protests on his behalf by the AA, the RAC or other motorist organisations acting macro-economically for millions are a second or seventh best sub-stitute. What is required is a method of direct pricing that reflects the wear, tear, congestion and other costs that individual motorists inflict on the roads and on other road users, and that induces road-suppliers to supply better roads at minimum cost.

The solution is to reproduce the taxi-meter: the micro-economic pricing device. No precise calculation may be possible because of the large element of overhead costs that have to be incurred for general maintenance whether an individual motorist uses the road or not, and because costs imposed on third-parties by congestion, etc. (exter-nalities) cannot easily be calculated. But there are some direct (marginal) costs that can be attributed to motorists for each unit of road used. Economists debate whether road-pricing should cover only marginal costs or also a share of overhead costs included in full, long-term average costs. But it seems that almost any price is better than no price at all, without which the motorist and road supplier are driving and building financially blind. The meter as the solution was

examined and recommended over ten years ago. [126] It could be the size
of a small book and form part of the number plate. It would clearly
cause motorists to rethink the amount and timing of their road use:
the charge could be varied to encourage them to shift from peak to
non-peak hours, crowded to uncrowded days, congested to un-
congested roads. And it would induce road suppliers to look to their
costs.

Street lighting

What about road lighting – in towns or on motorways? In towns it is
a public good. It is true that street lighting falls more on paths and
drives near lamps, but the cost of 'policing', recording, billing, etc.
would probably exceed the income from individual charges. Street
lighting is also a possible example of a public 'bad' – to people disturbed by light shining into bedrooms – and in principle would require
a reverse charge. Many government-controlled activities create public
'bads' – the noise of RAF aircraft on flightpaths, the noise from
motorways, the pollution of air and water by ordnance factories, the
traffic dislocation caused by Government receptions to VIP (or not-
so-important politicians), and so on.

Car parking

Meters are used increasingly for parking on the street or in car-parks.
But the charges for local government car parks do not generally cover
costs (Table C). Municipalities and councillors or officials that appeal
to external benefits shared by all citizens – for example, attraction of
visitors – should be required to replace vague assertions of 'benefits to
the town' by calculations of *how much* benefit goes to *whom*
(shop-keepers? restaurateurs? cinemas? betting-shops?) and show
why those who benefit should be subsidised by widows without cars,
pensioners, the lame and the halt who do not. They should be required
to show why parking charges should not cover the total costs incurred
by taxpayers. They do not because ratepayers passively accept their
rate burdens and few councillors do their job of representing their electors.

Is research a public good?

Government-financed research in medicine, armaments, etc. seems to
be a public good that bestows its benefits to all and sundry without

favour, because no one can be excluded physically or charged economically. Yet the economic analysis of research (that is, the production of information and knowledge) suggests a more refined approach.

The argument for financing research collectively by taxes is that it would not be undertaken by individuals because it cannot be charged for. Industry spends large sums on research to improve its products, methods, use of materials, and manpower, and 'charges' for it in the selling prices of its products. In so doing it showers externalities on everyone for many years ahead. The brain-scanner, which photographs 'slices' of the head and may benefit everyone for all time, was evolved by EMI after years of research. This is another example of the untold, incalculable, unintended externalities that are produced every day all over the world. It generally suffices for their immediate costs to be covered to ensure they are produced. Economists debate whether the basic source of innovation – the restless, inventive spirit of men and women – requires to be stimulated or rewarded by patents, copyrights or other exclusive rights to charge.[83, 84, 85] And rather shallow social scientists have claimed that the divergence that innovation opens up between private and social benefit destroys the argument for allowing individual researchers, inventors, scientists, etc. to pursue their genius; we should instead, it seems, direct them by officials who will calculate the incalculable by seeing the unseeable externalities. How far, then, is knowledge and information produced by 'pure' research – with no specific purpose but to explore the unknown – a public good that must be tax-financed because its beneficiaries cannot be charged?

No doubt there are such uncovenanted spin-offs from the advanced techniques used on atomic reactors, Concorde, the Rolls-Royce RB 211 engine, the vertical take-off Harrier, computers, and others. But the possibility of such externalities cannot be used to justify technical monstrosities such as giant aircraft or underwater mechanical brontosauri that might never cover their costs, especially if their opportunity costs in alternative use of resources thereby lost are taken into account – the improved living conditions, health care, help for pensioners and others who cannot help themselves, the arts, shorter working weeks to leave more leisure for reading and reflection. Enthusiasts for technical wonders can justify untold expenditure on the ground that externalities are *possible* that may benefit someone somewhere sometime. They can succeed more easily in their often euphoric but unsupported claims if the expenditure is public and the taxpayer who pays for it does not know enough to ask questions before it becomes politically irreversible (his 'representatives' in Parliament were no match for the informed officials and did not stop the Concorde extravaganza before it was too late). But that does not make government research and development a public good for which British taxpayers should pay.

First, if anyone anywhere may benefit some day, the money should come from taxpayers everywhere; so our government must induce other governments in every continent to contribute to the costs (to 'internalise' the externality on a world scale).[113] Second, it is dangerous to finance research and knowledge and scholarship from one source, political or private, because the unforeseen and unsought results may displease or damage the sponsor. So the sources of finance must be diversified: this is the strength of the privately-financed University College of Buckingham and of the Institute of Economic Affairs in contrast to state universities or research institutes that are almost wholly or very largely government-financed. Third, the political tax-financed sponsorship of research is more dangerous to its independence and objectivity than private sponsorship because political abuse (like the effort to direct scientists towards or away from an electorally sensitive subject) is more difficult to correct than abuse of private sponsorship.

The argument is thus for facilitating multiple sponsorship (by tax concessions for private research grants, as in the USA) rather than for tax-financing to encourage the externalities of government research. Because of the political popularity of giving public money for evidently 'good causes' or prestigious projects such as space and medical research, and the large claims made for them that are difficult to disprove by comparing costs and results, there has probably been too much tax-financed government-sponsored and too little privately-sponsored research. The externalities from tax financing are likely to have been over-stated and the externalities from private pricing (charges built into the selling prices of industrial products) under-developed.

Research is substantially a public good with potentially wide but unknowable externalities; but exclusive tax-financing of it is inferior to widespread price-financing encouraged by tax concessions. Private sponsors would be more sceptical of unsupported claims and more likely to require evidence of fruitful yields in terms of opportunity costs. When a physicist or sociologist asks for tax-money for research he should say 'If you give me the monetary value of a hospital or a school I *may* discover a new antibiotic or social habit, but your supporters are certain to lose their hospital or school.' And let the tax-paying public decide.

Personal social services

The official description 'personal social services' seems to be a contribution to confusion. It reflects the vagueness of government language. 'Social' means, if anything, shared; but 'personal' must mean not shared. Can anything be both?

The term is used for a range of services provided by local authorities to help people handicapped by age, incapacity, family difficulties, etc. – day nurseries, meals on wheels, home helps, and many more. Although they may yield external benefits they are not public goods in the essential economic sense because they can be – and are – given to individuals, and those who refuse to pay can be excluded. But the services are provided wholly or largely free. And here the term betrays a confusion that has fogged thinking about social policy in Britain for decades.

There is no dispute that people who cannot help themselves should be helped by those who can. That is common ground, and there is no excuse for the Child Poverty Action Group, Age Concern, or Shelter, or social workers or politicians to claim a corner in compassion. I argued earlier that we do not help people because they are old or disabled or widowed but because their age, disablement or widowhood prevents them helping themselves. That is why it has been such a tragic, callous mistake to make help available to all pensioners (millions of whom are well enough off), all the disabled (some of whom are well off), and all widows (some of whom are rich). The only criterion of entitlement to public help should be capacity for self-help, for which we use earnings as a broad measure. The balance of people who could help themselves but do not are the awkward squad of spongers who bring other recipients of help under suspicion.

Apart from the awkward squad, the criterion for social help should be, in practice, whether there is a shortage of earnings (or other income). If so, the case for help is made. But it does not follow that help should be given in kind – which means 'free'. Where there is physical or mental incapacity, help in kind may be best, or even necessary. Elsewhere it may be better to give cash – for all the reasons why it is better to provide services for a price rather than free. Help in kind teaches nothing and acclimatises its recipients to go on receiving it. Cash educates by its information, by teaching discrimination in choosing between alternatives, and by giving the recipient the status and dignity of the customer who pays in contrast to the supplicant who receives.

It must now be time, after decades of experience, to consider whether any of the help given by local authority 'personal social services' in kind could not be replaced by cash. The main ones are 'residential care', 'day care' (day nurseries, including play groups), 'community care' home helps, meals in the home. For some of these services there is a small charge. Cash grants or topping-up incomes to enable recipients to pay the charge would remove the sense of indebtedness. The benefit to the recipient is often clear enough. The obstruction would come from public employees who would lose their jobs or even voluntary workers who would lose their power.

There is probably even more argument for cash grants or reverse taxes to enable beneficiaries to pay for, or to pay the full cost of, local authority health services – health centres, mother/child clinics, midwifery, health visitors, home nursing, ambulances and possibly though less clearly family planning because of its externalities. In some circumstances a free or low-charge service may produce higher quality from dedicated social workers, nurses etc. who would prefer to be paid by the local authority than by the 'client' and thus feel they were 'giving' the service rather than selling it. But their feelings should come after those of their clients, who may prefer to pay as customers rather than receive as beneficiaries or supplicants.

Books, pictures, the arts

Free libraries, museums and art galleries are long overdue for payment by fees to cover part if not total costs. All are short of funds, though the suppliers and supporters of art and culture appear to prefer to importune politicians than to accept payment from their customers. Perhaps they think politicians can be persuaded to part with others' money more easily than customers with their own. But they must accept the consequences – battling it out in the press, Parliament and the Cabinet room where the outcome is more arbitrary than if the revenue of museums and art galleries were in part dependent on their popularity with the public. Even worse, as the doctors are finding at last; if you accept money from politicians you must also accept influence or control. And if you escape it, the politicians are not doing their duty by the public whose money they are giving away without anyone accounting for it.

Art and culture have widely dispersed externalities, but they are not public goods in the essential sense: they can be refused to people who refuse to pay. There may be room for paternalism and some tax-subsidy to bring some works of art to the public; how much is for the advocates to prove in terms of the alternatives sacrificed (like higher pensions for old people with low incomes). And it does not follow that there should be no charges at all. Countries like Holland, Italy and others that habitually charge have not killed off interest in art: their museums and art galleries seem to be used more generally than museums and art galleries in Britain. The relationship between price and demand may indeed be the opposite: I might have enjoyed the Constable exhibition at the Tate Gallery even more if I had paid £1 than I did at the free viewing shepherded by a Trustee.

At public libraries a 25p charge (cheap enough) for 600 million borrowings would yield around £150 million a year. This sum could fall to around £120 million if allowance were made for 10 per cent of borrowings by low-income pensioners and a further 10 per cent by children of low-income parents. Both groups could be excused payment by a certificate (as on the buses). Better still, they could be given earmarked purchasing power (a library voucher) or culture supplements with reverse taxes, so that they could pay along with everyone else, thus avoiding the nightmare of the sociologists – social divisiveness. This calculation supposes that borrowings do not fall away; but, if they do, they could hardly have been important to the borrowers.

Authors would be better advised to look for revenue from library charges than from government subsidies, and they should no more object to payment of fees by library borrowers than to payment of prices by book buyers.[30] In practice good writers would probably find it easier to get money out of readers than out of the government. They would certainly run no risk of political pressure. It is the library officials who are likely to obstruct charges, as administratively im-

practicable. They have no authority for obstructing them on poverty
or other grounds: that would be special pleading.

Information on jobs

Employment services may produce social (external) gains but they are
not a public good necessarily financed by taxes. There is little clear
thinking on the proportions in which job-finding should be paid for,
perhaps through insurance by the three parties involved: the government (to represent the externalities) employers and employees. The
retraining and other activities of the Manpower Commission are a
public good with externalities that government supplies in the effort to
offset the effects of its public bads like housing subsidies that discourage changing homes. Labour mobility is unavoidable in Britain
with its large dependence on overseas customers. On average people
change their jobs four or five times in a working life. A million people
change jobs each month. But still too many people will not move from
their districts – and still fewer from their homes. Subsidies tied to
housing must be blamed in part; trade union power to induce government to subsidise a failing firm is another culprit; and the Benn view
that firms fail because of poor management and can be saved by
worker control aided by a subsidy is a possible third. No wonder
government is now having to try harder to encourage men to change
jobs. But still it does not follow that employment or deployment services should be 'free'.

As with other government services, 'free' but passive government
employment exchanges have been increasingly deserted in favour of
priced but alert private agencies. One reason for the desertion is the
lack of funds to increase the efficiency of the exchanges and the lack
of incentive for the managers to improve them. Charges would help in
both.[27]

Until recent years the employment exchanges were used mostly by
wage-paid manual employees and were offering little competition to
the private agencies and their specialised skills in placing salaried,
professional, secretarial and nursing staffs. The employment exchanges have belatedly improved their own staffs and premises but
will have to do more to compete for salaried clients. Competition from
the private agencies has galvanised government to supplement its
employment exchanges by more business-like Job Centres, although
charges may be necessary to convey the spirit of a skilled service

designed for individual clients rather than a social service for national insurance beneficiaries. And again the intention of government to remove competition by licensing and restricting the private agencies is suppressing a symptom (under the pretext of anxiety to prevent the agencies' over-activity in encouraging mobility) that will reappear in other forms unless the government service is improved. And that is unlikely on the required scale as long as it remains a 'social' service given free (for taxes) and fails to transform itself into a personal service sold for fees.

The doubt remains whether a service managed by state officials and bureaucratic procedures can change its nature. At least charging would give it the best opportunity of discovering its potentialities. In that event it would also have to segregate its 'social' functions of paying unemployment and other social benefits.

Water and sewage

Charges for delivering water to industry and for collecting sewage may seem more familiar. Malvern has long had a metered supply of water. And a House of Lords decision has required local authorities to return a proportion of rates to ratepayers not on main drainage. Charging for both these services would have the advantages of information, economy, consumer alertness, cost consciousness, potential competition; it seems hardly necessary to argue it further. The opposition to charging is based not so much on reasoning as on inertia and conservatism.

School meals, 'welfare' foods

Charging the full cost of school meals, milk and welfare is more controversial because it is in the 'social' sphere where it is thought that some parents are destitute, irresponsible, or ignorant. Even if these accusations were well-founded about enough parents to justify free meals, etc. for the children of all parents, including most who are not destitute, irresponsible or ignorant, this policy would not remove the supposed shortcomings. Free or subsidised meals do not teach parents to be less destitute, less irresponsible or less ignorant. A gradual change to cash, or in the early stages to vouchers for meals, milk and welfare foods, would restore or create the sense of responsibility for a child's well-being, not least by putting parents with cash or vouchers on the same economic footing as parents who paid.

Sports and recreation

There remains a wide range of sports and recreation facilities and amenities – from swimming (and washing) baths to 'free' beaches.

Government baths for washing and baths for swimming have been paid for by rates (and taxes) for over a century.[49] They originated in the Public Health Acts of the 1850s and 1860s which authorised local authorities to provide them out of taxes. The main impulse was the hope of improving personal hygiene as a safeguard against contagion or infection in the growing cities with primitive sanitation and drainage. Poverty – the inability to pay – was a supporting reason. Insofar as everyone benefited by cleanliness in everyone else, so that the benefit was inseparable, such amenities contained an element of public goods. With generally low incomes it was easy to argue for financing through rates and taxes, though it was (indirect) taxes themselves that partly made people too poor to pay – the same circular reasoning as in the argument for free education.

Gradually baths were followed by other amenities and facilities. A century after the Public Health Acts local authorities are still providing 'free' (or with charges that do not cover costs so that they are wholly or partly financed by taxes) a wide range of amenities from children's play gardens to golf courses. The whole structure was formalised in 1965 when control passed from the Department of Education and Science to the Sports Council, with nine regional councils to make grants to local activities. In 1972 the task was given to the local authorities.

The supposition implied in the emerging political creation of sports and recreation facilities as a function of government is that people would not wish to play or watch sport unless stimulated by government; or that, if they did, they would not be able to pay to attract resources from other activities. Here as elsewhere, these and other of the five ancillary reasons – that government would build on a large scale and therefore more cheaply, etc. – have been called in to justify a growing structure of 'public' services for which people must pay by taxes. In 1971 the Sports Council estimated that some £300 million to £400 million would be required in tax funds in the ten years to 1981 for indoor swimming pools and sports centres, for golf courses, and for other facilities. It said there was 'a need for local authorities to take the initiative on an increasing scale to provide sports facilities for the community'.[127] In 1973 a Select Committee of the House of Lords showed its concern by proposing that the new District Councils in the reorganisation of local government should have a Recreation Department and a Chief Executive. This proposal had in principle been anticipated by the Durham and Teesside Authority, which had established a Department of Arts and Recreation 'to co-ordinate and combine leisure activities', and had 'co-ordinated' and 'combined' theatres and libraries with playing fields and sports centres. An early product was Thornaby Pavilion, said to be 'a unique approach to leisure ... a place to practise one's interests in a social setting'.

Sport, recreation, leisure amenities are, like health and education, commonly thought to be clearly desirable 'good things'. Especially if their tax-costs, and, even more, their opportunity costs in roads or police manning, etc., are overlooked, they must be a tempting way for local politicians to combine 'doing good' with enhancing their chances of returning to office at municipal elections (to go on doing more good). Here the economist, like the doctor who identifies over-indulgence as a cause of obesity and prescribes commonsense avoidance of fattening foods as its cure, is apt to attract dislike for pointing to the link between cause and result. The economist also has to add a dash of clear thinking that is the essence of economic theorising. If sport and recreation are 'good things' in themselves, there is no limit to the lengths that local government should go in providing them. £20,000 is then well spent on a wave-making machine for Nottingham Council's municipal swimming pool: better than still water, it would teach Nottingham children to cope with the currents of the real sea. Still better, imported sharks would teach them to resist the dangers of the deep. And so on, *ad infinitum*. The costs to the balance of payments would be remote from the ratepayer's and taxpayer's attention, and no politician would disturb the euphoria by emphasising it.

These examples may seem grotesque. On the contrary, they are logical extensions of the view that people should swim in realistic conditions, that swimming is a public good from which all may benefit by the increase in potential life-savers, and that it is therefore proper for government to encourage swimming by providing it partly free. They also illustrate the grotesqueries that could follow as more services are financed communally by taxes without the individual awareness of cost that comes with charging, and therefore without calculation or even recognition of opportunity costs. The concept of externalities as used by economists is carefully defined as uncovenanted effects on third parties. When used loosely and vaguely by politicians and sociologists it can appear to justify unending use of resources on activities that would reduce living standards by yielding benefits that the people – for whom, after all, they are intended – have not said they want at the costs that would be entailed. The Sports Council said in 1973 that sports centres are desirable 'to avert social and medical ills'. So are eating and sleeping: that is no reason for supplying food and water-beds on the rates. The economist is not satisfied with only one side of the account; he wants to know, or rather he says the people must know, the other side before investment in Sports Centres can be justified. And they cannot know unless there are charges to indicate costs and the alternatives sacrificed.

I rather like the idea that people who lightly claim public money for this, that or the other good cause should have a personal stake and pay a penalty if the benefit does not materialise.

There is not much time to lose. By 1974, 265 sports centres were open or being built in England and Wales; by 1981, 815 will have been built if the Sports Council has its way. So far the shortfall between expenditure and revenue has been commonly between £50 and £100 million. (In 1973-4 it was £88,000 in Guildford, £231,000 in Bracknell.)

The poor benefit less than the rich

Much the same is true in general principle of other 'public' sports and recreational facilities. An irony is that the 'social' justification of a century ago has been turned on its head. These 'public' services were then supposed to have been provided by government because they were a way to transfer income from the rich (who paid the taxes) to the poor (who enjoyed the bathing and the swimming). It seems that now, a century later, half of the adults who use the sport facilities regularly (twice or thrice a month) come from the upper and middling income groups; a third of swimmers from the highest income groups.[49] Another study found that only a quarter were 19 years of age and younger (mostly in table tennis, trampoline and judo); two-thirds were aged 20 to 40 (mostly squash, badminton, sauna).

A charge, of course, reduces demand by acting as a 'barrier', as the price-less sociologists like to put it, or more correctly as a reminder of the resources used in production by the supplier and the alternatives foregone by the buyer. How much it will deter demand is measured by the 'elasticity'. Some people will be deterred strongly: they prefer something else. Others may not be deterred very much, if at all: they want to pay the higher price and sacrifice the alternative. How much higher charges would diminish the use of sports facilities is for experience to reveal. In squash it seems that the higher charges at sports centres do not discourage users.[49] The reason may be the relatively high income of squash players or the popularity of the game that stimulated the wide development of private courts charging prices that cover the full costs, so that squash-players are accustomed to pay them. And this strong demand has evidently enabled sports centres to charge prices around double those for badminton, basketball, cricket (nets), five-a-side football, and golf.

But the rate-payers continue to pay heavily for public swimming pools. In 1974-5 local rate-payers, whether they used the pools or not, paid around £50 million; swimmers paid about £15 million. The Sports Council judged in 1972 that 411 indoor pools were 'required' in England by 1981 (including replacing a third of old pools, many built before 1900) at a capital cost of £58 million. Few pools cover their costs (including interest on loans). The loss ranges up to a quarter of a million pounds per pool.[49] If state schools had to cover their costs they would soon find ways to make their pools pay. (They too are subsidised by rate-payers under the heading of education.)

Charges for a 'public' service are sometimes varied according to ability to pay. This variation is confusing to supplier and buyer because it obscures the information conveyed by price, which is that a stated amount of resources has been used, whether by poor pensioner or rich pop-singer. It is therefore better to vary the element of *topping up* so that everyone can pay the *same* price. (This is also the argument against varying prescription charges with income.) In some circumstances it may nevertheless be administratively simpler to vary the price. Two out of three users of new pools (built since 1960) are children. Half of the adults are 'skilled manual workers' but a third come from the highest incomes. Between half and two-thirds go as families.[49] Only 1 in 20 go professionally; the other 19 go for recreation. (The pools at Bletchley and Heringthorpe Leisure Centres have artificial palm trees as well as wave machines.) It may be that cunning (but concealed) calculations have divined that the externalities of swimming are especially high and that swimmers are more worthy or deserving of tax-subsidies than other pleasure-seekers. But none of these wholesome, health-giving recreations is a public good that cannot be refused to people who refuse to pay; and all yield private benefits that should not be subsidised by people who cannot or do not enjoy them.

Parks and open spaces

Parks and open spaces may be public goods because, although individuals can be excluded, the cost of collecting entrance fees may exceed the income. The cost to tax-payers in 1975–6 was over £100 million. If admission charges are uneconomic, income could perhaps be drawn from park-users in other ways. In North Yorkshire the persistence of a principled Councillor (Chapter 12) has persuaded the Council to provide more informative guides to the Yorkshire dales and to charge for them, thus changing an expenditure borne by ratepayers generally into a surplus. The leaflets were also used more considerately rather than forming litter. (Predictably the reform was opposed by. the bureaucracy.)

For sports and recreation generally, charges would increase income and so provide the resources for improved services and, moreover, help to indicate more precisely which services the public wanted. They are used by one in four of the population, mostly by people with higher incomes. In evidence to the Layfield committee on local government, Mr Alan Jenkins, an economist with specialised knowledge of the sports industry, judged that charges could be raised by an average of 25p at sports centres and swimming pools.[49] This would mean doubling or even trebling them, and would close the wide gap between costs and charges. The higher charges would help to take the facilities out of politics and enable the managers to adapt them more closely to public preferences without the arbitrary fluctuations in policies and funds produced by the party pendulum. Not least, they would avoid the tragi-comic use (as in medical care, education, etc.) of nil or low charges (squash 10p instead of 60p) in the vain hope of making a service available to all and ending by making it available to none – except at lower standards because tax-funds fail to fill the gap between cost and income.

Seaside facilities

Recreational facilities in seaside resorts also show the scope for improvement by charging, or by charging nearer cost. The range is from
beach charges and boat licences to deck chair and cabin fees.[80] Like
museum and art gallery charges, they are common in Holland, Italy
and other countries on the Continent, whose tourists in Britain often
find lower standards for which the low (or nil) charge is no compensa-
tion since they would rather pay for something better. The closer comparison by British and overseas holidaymakers with other countries
(and the competition from them) is itself a reason for charging for
facilities in Britain to raise revenue for improvement. Only the natives
suffer from indifferent refuse collection in Ruislip or ill-stocked
libraries in Lowestoft, but the balance of payments suffers if overseas
tourists are repelled by rubbish-strewn beaches or poor boating
facilities.

Here again, as elsewhere, there are errors and attitudes that
obstruct reform. The notion that beaches are 'public' property that
should be provided 'free' dies hard. It overlooks their scarcity: good
beaches are not merely spaces lapped by the tide but also with comfortable surfaces, patrolled by beach-keepers, periodically tidied,
protected from high wind, facing south, near hotels or caravan sites —
but not so near as to attract over-crowding and the inevitable and
irksome, time-wasting rationing device of queuing. If price is not used
they will tend to be unkempt, and crowded. Like other 'public' services, they will end up 'free' but undesirable, because they will not
offer the quality that people want, can pay for and are accustomed to
in services for which they are pleased to pay elsewhere. Again, the
fallacy that a public service paid for by taxes is somehow intrinsically
better than a private service sold for a price obstructs clear thinking.
Charging would encourage beach suppliers to meet the users' requirements, perhaps by inducing local authorities to farm them out to
private, competitive, beach amenity specialists rather than leave them
to be run by town hall officials.

Of 3,000 miles of British coastline, only a third is beach owned by
local authorities, of which about a half is commonly preferred by
holidaymakers. Since there are no charges (for people on foot), rationing is enforced by 'first come, first served', as in the NHS or public
libraries, or by queuing, as with public conveniences, or by subterfuge

and black markets, like crossing the palm of the deck-chair attendant, as with Council housing. The moral question is whether these forms of rationing are less objectionable than charging. The public can be guided to less frequented beaches by paternalistic placing of beach shops, cafes, car parks and other amenities, but there is still rationing: there is no escaping scarcity.

The virtue of the tax-paid system, which forces most people into a quality of beach that is either higher or, more generally, lower then they would prefer, is not readily clear. What is clear is that British beaches offer no choices between lower-quality free beaches and higher quality priced beaches; and the one quality offered is lower than available in countries with charges. Yet charges for deck-chairs and wind-breaks, or for storing and launching boats, are administratively simple. Differential charges for chalets and huts provoke no bureaucratic barrier. People with their own chairs or tents can be charged for use of the space they occupy. Since these are not characteristically bureaucratic services, they might be made to yield revenue by the sale of franchises or concessions to private firms.

It may not be apparent to the casual or even periodic user that beaches are not natural features but require maintenance of sea walls, groynes, promenades, shelters and so on. If the income is inadequate (or used inefficiently), maintenance can be postponed, but with gradual deterioration and inconvenience (or danger) to the public.

Boating is an increasingly popular sport that could not have been foreseen a century ago, and there is no reason why errors and attitudes must persist when conditions change. Speed-boats, usually carried by trailer and sometimes launched from beaches, compete for space and cause congestion. They could yield increasing revenue in launching and mooring fees. Fishing rights carry charges, but often low or nominal.

Piers and harbours, like car-parking, can be said to attract visitors whose purchasing power benefits local traders, and it may be argued that their charges should therefore not have to cover their costs. The probability is that the external benefits are over-estimated, so local rate-payers are over-taxed and users under-charged. Direct charges are more likely to provoke protest if they are raised or seem high, but rate-payers can rarely argue back at Councillors who speak vaguely about the importance of providing 'public' services that attract visitors, although many of these Councillors are shopkeepers or hoteliers. Such claims are rarely accompanied by statistics that can be challenged. Local traders who benefit personally from visitors should pay for the public services that attract them.

Seaside entertainment provided by local authorities is another public service it is tempting to justify as attracting visitors and thus properly paid for by uncomplaining rate-payers. Here the reluctance to raise charges nearer costs can create a vicious circle. Low charges bring inadequate revenue which is met by reducing outlays. Falling quality then reduces revenue further. Higher charges could be the way to improve quality and raise revenue to cover costs.

Decorative illuminations seem to be an obvious public good from which non-payers cannot be excluded and which should therefore be financed by the rates. Scarborough has charged for its Wonderland Display but all visitors to Blackpool can see its illuminations. Bands can be heard over a wide radius at Folkestone, Bournemouth and Colwyn Bay, but charges can be made to enter the 'stands' for better hearing. (That these patrons may often be pensioners is not a reason for low charges that subsidise affluent pensioners and non-pensioners but for vouchers or reverse taxes to top up the low incomes of non-affluent pensioners.)

A close observer, W. D. Peppiatt – a school-teacher of economics who is also a Councillor in Thanet,[80] has concluded that conventional seaside charging is inadequate on five main grounds: the revenue falls short of costs; it does not efficiently equate supply and demand; revenue from local rates or government grants is insufficient for capital outlays; congestion in the short peak season alternates with under-use during the rest of the year; seasides have failed to provide the sophisticated services expected both by British holiday-makers accustomed to higher standards abroad and by overseas tourists bringing their currencies to succour the ailing balance of payments. The ultimate solution is charges as the alternative to further support from rates or taxes. Otherwise British seasides may deteriorate progressively, as is seen by occasional abandonment of facilities such as the West Pier at Brighton, or the increase in private provision, as in the new Marina also at Brighton. There has been a lopsided persistence in older amenities (such as entertainments) because they do not require much capital expenditure and a failure to develop new facilities that do (boat moorings, etc.).

This imbalance of supplies and demands is a not unexpected result of failure to use price to equate them. Charges nearer costs would help to right the imbalance. Higher launching fees and mooring charges and perhaps an annual boat fee would yield revenue to improve harbours. New (or higher) charges varying with beach amenities would reduce congestion and enable beaches to be cleaned and patrolled.

In a word, there has been little logic about the haphazard mixture of rates, taxes and charges that have financed – or failed to finance – the varied services of the British seaside. It is the outcome of outdated conditions, chance, expediency, habit, tradition, prejudice, error and conservatism. And much the same is true of all or most of the other 'public' services. They are all hallowed by time, sanctified by usage; and if that is how we want them so we shall have them. But indulgence in this mixed bag of nostalgia demands a high cost: the neglect of facilities the public would prefer and would enjoy if it were allowed to pay charges instead of being confined to the outdated method of taxes.

9 From coal to clean air

The last five chapters reviewed activities that, for a century, government has increasingly argued are 'public' or social services which should not be sold commercially as in a market but should be provided wholly or largely 'free'. This chapter discusses more summarily services that government provides usually not as public or social services but as trading or commercial services; and the question is whether the charges should cover cost. Some are supplied by local government, others through organisations that used to be known as 'public utilities' and in recent years as 'public corporations'.

Local government trading services

The local government services are a mixed bag from restaurants to crematoria. To see how far they are, in practice, supplied as trading services that cover their costs and stand on their own feet rather than on the ratepayers' corns, I listed them earlier in Table C and showed their cost (expenditure) and receipts from fees, charges and sales. We saw that incomes were much higher as percentages of cost (government expenditure) than for the 'social' services, national and local. Some were in the eighties but others lagged far behind. Before we ask why taxpayers have to pay even for trading services, let us recall from Table C what they are and how much is still found by taxes.

If the official statistics mean what they say, it would seem that in a recent year we were paying in taxes not only for public (or social) services but also, in large part, for 'trading' services that local government sells in return for payment, as in private industry. Municipal aerodromes cost £20 million (in 1973-4) but drew only £12 million in charges and left ratepayers and taxpayers to find the rest – £8 million. Horticultural markets cost £3 million but drew only £1 million in charges, leaving £2 million to ratepayers and taxpayers. Slaughterhouses cost £6 million, earned £3 million and received £3 million from the rates and taxes. And so on.

Should taxpayers pay for private benefits?

None of these services is a public good in the sense that it cannot be denied to individuals who will not pay. Indeed there were charges for all of them. There must be reasons why the charges do not cover costs.

As we have seen, it is easy to argue that a local government service, such as an aerodrome, benefits the town as a whole and should therefore be financed partly by local taxpayers. That argument could justify every town impoverishing its people to supply visitors with free transport, entertainment, restaurants and hotels, *ad infinitum*, for imponderable benefits. Politically powerful groups like officials, contractors who hope for contracts, or organised employees may benefit, but the town, its government and its taxpayers have to consider whether the subsidy to visitors could be used better in other ways. If these subsidies to local trading services with undefined and uncalculated externalities continue, it may be simply that local taxpayers have not noticed them, because the cost to each taxpayer is small and tucked away in total expenditure figures that he cannot investigate, or because his elected representatives in the town hall have failed to represent him.

Whatever the reasons, the not generally known and surprising truth seems to be that slaughterhouses, markets, cemeteries, corporation estates, industrial estates, ports and piers, etc. are evidently paid for in part by local rate payers who do not use them. Do they know? Do their representatives tell them? Is that what they want? Is it too difficult or costly to find out for themselves? Are there remedies? Or is the empire-building by local councillors and officials too powerful?

If it is thought these services should be subsidised by ratepayers, they should not be classified as 'trading' services. And if local government is careless in running trading services inefficiently, so that charges do not cover costs, perhaps they should have them run by more efficient managers. In the meantime it is not difficult to see why rates are high. It has evidently been too easy to load the costs on to ratepayers, who are many, so that the cost per head is small (and will be concealed in the rate demand notice). Although local taxes have been rising for a century, ratepayers do not examine their rate demands as closely as their butchers', bakers' or garage bills. If they did, and were shocked, they cannot individually escape paying rates except by moving or emigrating. Their collective revolt of recent years, and their continuing passive resistance by late payment, was provoked by the dramatic increase in the nominal number of pounds demanded due to inflation, not by reading the rate demand notice and asking whether local services were worth the rate bill. In any event, to judge value for money, ratepayers would have to know the value of services and costs to them individually, which would require full charging.

The official statistics suggest that if charges for local government trading services covered their costs, rates and taxes in 1973-4 could have been reduced by about £500 million (item 3, fourth column of figures in Table C, assuming overhead costs were accurately allocated to individual services).

Public corporations

Trading services supplied on a national scale by public corporations are more familiar because they are larger, and they have been the focus of political controversy by being nationalised. (One of them, indeed – steel – has been denationalised and renationalised, and another – the Post Office – changed from a government department to a supposedly independent corporation.) Also, they impinge on daily lives more than little-noticed slaughterhouses, which seem to have come down from the distant past, or the aerodromes that Councillors may, like the politicians of developing countries who build air-strips, regard as prestigious symbols of status.

Whether public services should be paid for collectively by taxes or individually by charges is the central controversy over the running and financing of the public corporations producing fuel, transport, steel, broadcasting and other communications. They accounted for 16 per cent of the GNP and 8 per cent of the labour force in 1974, and since then we must add British Leyland and other undertakings 'taken over' by government. They are described variously as Councils, Boards, Corporations, Executives, Authorities, Groups, even Companies. Ideally they should be free of political control, so that they can concentrate on efficiency in adapting themselves to changes in technology and consumer preferences in market conditions. For various reasons – at best because they have high degrees of monopoly, arguably because they can be used in macro-economic management to keep the official price index down, at worst because they can be used by government in its electoral tactics of creating jobs and buying votes – they are supervised by Ministers 'in the public interest'. Their orders from government have varied from injunctions to act commercially and cover costs to requests, sometimes backed by subsidies, to keep their prices down in the hope of limiting the inflationary rises in the cost of living, especially for people with low incomes, and persuading trade unions to restrain their wage demands in operating incomes policies.

Beyond these diverse tactical government objectives there is the over-riding philosophic question whether the Corporations are selling their products at a price to cover costs or supplying them as social services, for which prices are secondary, irrelevant or objectionable, as has been argued for rail and bus transport. Before he resigned from the British Railways Board, Sir Richard Marsh indicated fairly plainly that it was difficult for him (or anyone else) to run the railways effectively if the government did not know its own mind, or changed it unpredictably between the two philosophies – tactically to meet current economic problems like inflation or strategically to meet the changing balance of power in the governing political party.

The central theme of this book is thus at the heart of the dispute over the role and function of the government-supervised (if not government-directed) industries that supply the basic commodities of fuel and steel, the basic services of transport and communications, and the jugular vein of an open society, broadcasting.

Monopoly and externality

There are two complex issues affecting charging. First, the public corporations run industries in which, it is argued, there is a large element of heavy investment and equipment. This makes very large units, which can offer the economies of scale, necessary for efficiency (which may be true, as in steel, but not always). There cannot therefore be many producing organisations, so there is the possibility and danger of monopoly. Second, these industries are said to have large externalities so that they should not be run commercially to cover costs but should reflect wider social repercussions.

Recent governments have therefore evolved the policy that their prices should be equated with marginal costs: the direct costs of producing the 'last' unit, not the full average costs which include an allocation of overhead costs. Other economists have argued[86, 87] that this is an artificial application of the pricing policy that emerges spon-

taneously in competitive markets where firms try to maximise the surplus of revenue over costs, i.e. their profits. Since the public corporation industries are not necessarily monopolies but could operate in
competitive markets if restrictions on competition from new forms of
fuel, transport and communication were removed, the better policy
would be to remove these obstacles and to leave them to make the
charges required to maximise their profits by covering their costs.

Second, if charges are to be decided or guided by analyses of external or social costs and benefits, estimates of the benefits to third parties would be required. But, as indicated earlier, these estimates are in
practice very crude and little more than rough and arbitrary guesses.
There is really no convincing way of measuring external benefits (or
detriments) imposed on third parties except by confronting them with
a series of prices and seeing how they react in the real world. The Vic-
toria line in London reduces congestion on the roads, but the value of
the easier movement from avoiding delay could be discovered only by
finding how much travellers would pay for, say, faster buses. So again
it would seem better to leave the corporations, like private firms, to
charge what they think necessary to maximise their profits, but in as
competitive a market as possible.

If this procedure left some people with inadequate transport, and it
was thought desirable that they should remain where they are rather
than move, they could be given individual grants so that they could
pay the charges. Again as before, the special assistance is better given
on the demand side, at the expense of the country as a whole, than on
the supply side by fares too low to cover costs and therefore at the expense of the industry.

More simply, the supply of transport in, say, rural areas where
public transport is inadequate or expensive, could be increased by
allowing car-owners to charge for lifts or private coach-owners to
compete with nationalised road and rail transport. This solution would
require little more than the removal of restrictions on competition.
These restrictions are made by man — politicians and bureaucrats, not
by nature. Many commuters could travel more cheaply by private
coach than by nationalised train. And competition would turn the
railways from devising fare increases to internal cost reductions.

Finance by charging in competitive conditions
There is thus no difference in principle between charging in public cor-

porations and in industry in general. And basically the reason is that
public corporations are operating increasingly, and could be made to
operate even more, in competitive conditions.

Unfortunately the official statistics conceal rather than reveal how
far charges cover costs. There are direct subsidies in the form of
money transferred to pay costs (British Rail has received around £500
million a year and in 1968 wrote off £1,250 million of capital as a
dead loss). There are also indirect subsidies in the form of protection
from competition, both from inside Britain (restrictions on Laker
Airways, road hauliers, etc.) and from outside (tariffs on imported oil
and coal). The discouragement of competition has probably bloated
costs, so that the subsidy is larger than it otherwise would be. The
Post Office, for example, has continued postal services long after they
were uneconomic. Without the effective discouragement of bankrupt-
cy to prove them wrong, public corporations can find imposing social
reasons for continuing services they cannot make pay by charging to
cover costs.

What is clear is that these deficits might have been less if the Corporations had been left to adjust their prices to their costs and if costs
had been exposed to more competitive conditions. Government policy
could then have been directed, first, to preventing costs from being inflated by removing the obstacles to competition rather than con-
solidating them and, second, confining assistance to individuals, such
as pensioners, who would have suffered hardship from paying, say,
the whole cost of their fuel and transport. A general directive that the
Corporations must also cover their costs without subsidy might have
helped to prevent those costs from being pushed up by trade unions,
which under the present system are in a dominating bargaining position in wage negotiation and in obstructing the pruning of uneconomic
railway lines and stations, coalpits, bus routes, etc. Governments are
not as effective in restraining these extravaganzas as the prospect of
having to close down because competitors are more efficient.

Allowing the Corporations to vary their charges in a more competitive environment, and with selective assistance for the low-income
consumers, could thus have avoided many of the wastes, excesses and
distortions in these basic industries and services. Some government
attention would still be required, because for a time some of the services provided might be able to make their charges higher than their
costs because of a degree of monopoly. But the monopoly has been

crumbling in all of them – fuel, transport, steel, communications and broadcasting – and it would have crumbled even faster if competition had been welcomed rather than discouraged or suppressed. In broadcasting – 'pay-TV', in postal services – private carriers, in transport – toll roads, in fuel – North Sea oil, and in steel and coal – imports: these are examples of potential competition that has been inhibited or held at bay. Until competition is allowed it cannot be argued that the Corporations have an *unavoidably* high degree of monopoly such that they cannot be allowed to vary their charges without political control. More competition would by now have reduced costs in all of them. It would have induced the Post Office to mechanise sorting, cut out twice daily or weekend delivery (or better still require higher charges). It would have compelled British Rail to cut its 11,000 miles to the 6,000 or 7,000 used by passengers prepared to pay enough in fares without expecting others to pay part of their fares in taxes. More flexible fares could have evened out the daily, weekly and seasonal fluctuations in travel instead of intensifying them. In fuel, more competition would have pruned staffs, galvanised selling techniques and improved sensitivity to consumer requirements. If not, the public corporations would gradually have been replaced by private firms providing better services at lower cost. (Professor Milton Friedman says his son, David Friedman, has discovered that government services usually cost twice as much as private competitive services).[26]

Not least, all the Corporations would benefit in their capital-raising by being provided with a trading framework in which their more competitive (more commercial, less political) charging would more quickly identify which of their activities were profitable, in growing demand, and should be expanded, and which were in declining demand, making losses, and should be shut down. But as long as the public corporations can look to politicians and taxes to make up for low charges they can hardly be expected to put the public first.

The conclusion is that, as elsewhere, charging should be used as much, not as little, as possible, to cover costs.

Paying for the environment

There remain government services that create the environment for human activity, and government measures to optimise the use of the environment (air, water, etc.) in human activity.

Insofar as environmental and preventive services are public goods, such as measures to contain contagious or infectious diseases, they should be financed by taxes, since everyone benefits by everyone else being treated, including those who refuse to take part or to pay. Even here, however, there is room for a charge. Individuals who are treated would benefit even if others were not; and if it was thought that some individuals would be foolhardy and put both themselves and others at risk, preventive measures could be required by law if enough citizens (a majority? two-thirds? three-quarters? 95 per cent with a veto by 5 per cent?) agreed.[114]

Coast and bird protection, conservation of areas of natural beauty by national or countryside parks, preservation of buildings of historic interest, safeguarding of works of art and the preservation of civilised life itself may be substantially public goods that would not be produced at all unless produced for all and paid for collectively by taxes. They yield benefits to everyone in the area; increased use by some does not reduce use by others; they cannot be refused to individuals; charges cannot be levied.

At least, so say people who would like to see these activities paid for by others. But not everyone is a bird-watcher, a visitor to stately homes, or a fresh-air fiend. The argument, here as elsewhere, can easily be overdone, and the opportunity costs conveniently overlooked. Culture is a good to be preserved, but should the uncultured pay for the cultured? Should working-class soccer fans pay for middle-class opera-goers? And what about the opportunity costs? How many museums for how many hospitals?

Moreover, amenities are not all necessarily best provided without direct charge to anyone. Especially where congestion is possible or likely, as in beaches or stately homes, charges may be practicable and advantageous. A flexible method might be *voluntary* charging such as at the Chicago Art Institute, which is 'free' but which suggests donations that individuals may care to make. But compulsory partial charging is better.

Even where 'free rides' are unavoidable and charging is impracticable, tax-financing and 'free' provision embodies the defect that there is no sensitive indicator of the *scale* on which public goods should be protected, conserved or safeguarded. Do we spend too little tax-money on coast protection or on bird sanctuaries, or too much? Do we spend too much on the Tate Gallery, or too little? Is there a tragic loss of Tudor mansions, or a surfeit? The scope for error, favouritism, corruption that is inherent in the political method of control of free public goods may make it the second best. An even better instrument might be one in which individuals could indicate the strengths of their personal preferences through pricing. Referenda are again a possible method. In a Virginia county recently the people voted against a new (tax-financed) courthouse. Referenda are frequent in Swiss cantons. Town meetings are another possibility, reminiscent of the direct democracies of the Greek city states.

Finally, parts of the environment may require protection, not from neglect but from over-use. Here there are several main elements in the argument.[1] The environment is partly unprotected where it is unappropriated by any owner and thus *really* free (no quotation marks): no-one owns it, so no-one ensures that it is not despoiled. Again, the purpose is not to prevent all pollution but to optimise it, where a little of the environment (clean air, water, etc.) can be used to make a lot of goods and services to raise living standards. Further, the environment is polluted by government as well as by private industry, and in communist as well as in capitalist countries. Not least, the better method of protection may be not by outright prohibition but by charges to reveal preferences and discourage over-use (pollution) and to stimulate the search for methods to reduce both. Pricing the environment can thus be a more effective way of protecting it than direct government regulation or prohibition, which provides no measure of the cost of the environment used or polluted, and no incentive to reduce its pollution.

Charging for the environment is the means of conserving it. There is thus a case for charging even where it might be thought least applicable.

Resistance to reform

If the advantages of charging are so plain, why are charges absent or inadequate? The answer must be that there are no incentives to charge to cover costs, or that there are incentives *not* to charge to cover costs. Charging puts the suppliers – politicians and bureaucrats – face to face with the customers who feel the power of people who pay, who know they pay, and who know how much they pay. Politicians and bureaucrats have a more comfortable (because less demanding) and more powerful (because less accountable) life when the customers are more distant, less informed and less well-placed to complain – that is, when they pay by taxes. Resources can then be used more as politicians and bureaucrats think fit, and less as the awkward paymaster-customers want. That is why we must expect politicians and bureaucrats to prefer indirect payment by taxes, to look askance at direct payment by charges, and to do what they can to resist it. They are not selfless paragons. They are men with personal interests – from families to philosophies – to serve. That does not make them morally worse than the rest of us, but it means we cannot assume that they are necessarily better. They erect a real, formidable resistance to reform. They have a direct, personal interest in keeping the government, that is, the tax-paid sector, as large as possible. This means they support the inefficient use of resources in all public services that are not public goods. The arguments they use to defend their position are the subject of the next part of this book.

PART 3

Objections Overruled

10 Socially undesirable

This and the following two chapters will consider the three main objections to charging directly for the separable private benefits in public services. This chapter discusses the view that it is socially unacceptable.

The social objections are of five main kinds:

First, people and their needs come before paying and prices. Mankind is more important than money; adequate health, decent housing, good education and other essentials are man's birthright, which it is objectionable and obscene to submit to commercial calculus.

Second, poor people cannot pay charges.

Third, some people who could pay would not pay for good housing, health, etc., because they preferred less important things.

Fourth, charging might in time require people to choose between different suppliers, political and/or commercial, who would persuade them against their best interests.

Fifth, charging would be socially divisive. Each individual (family) would think of himself (itself) rather than of society; in contrast, sharing in public services for which we all pay by taxation is socially cohesive.

Compassion and cost

The social objections to charging – particularly that the poor cannot pay – are the most difficult to discuss rationally because they are advanced for emotional as well as logical reasons. It is easy for the opponents of charging to make themselves seem to be on the side of the angels: compassionate, caring, concerned for the poor, the halt, the lame, the sick, the blind, the fatherless, the deserted, the neglected, the bashed and in general the downtrodden, the under-privileged and the disadvantaged. Conversely it is easy to make the advocates of charging appear cold, callous, unfeeling, hard-hearted. The late Professor Richard M. Titmuss, a leader of the post-war thinking that favoured 'free' social services, commonly made his adversaries appear to be not only wrong but also immoral. He, and two other writers nearest to him, Professor Peter Townsend and (rather less so) Professor Brian Abel-Smith, wrote in the cadences of compassion, almost as spokesmen for the underdog, and often with more than a hint that their adversaries were more interested in economic systems, or even commercial interests, than in people, especially the poor.

As a participant in the post-war controversy with the senior trio of welfare sociologists, Titmuss, Townsend and Abel-Smith, I often sensed the accusation of callousness. I always thought they were do-ing no service to clear thinking to obscure it with emotional specula-tion about motive, but I tried to see whether there was substance in their emotionalism. Such writers seem to think that economists who analyse social policies in terms of their costs and prices, supply and demand, profit and loss, must put people and their needs second. The characteristic sociological feeling is that the economist's study of (or emphasis on) costs and payment is commercial, materialistic, mercenary, grubby. (I use sociological to mean relating to society or groups, mostly large groups, rather than to individuals: 'pensioners' rather than George Baker, retired bookkeeper, bookbinder, bookseller, bookmaker. . . . In this sense sociology is a macro-study and makes the same mistakes as macro-economics that forgets its micro-economic components.)

This paternalistic disdain for the choices of ordinary men in the market can be rationalised as compassion. And there may be the view that the economist is hard-hearted in his persistence with the fun-damental and unavoidable truth that people must pay in one way or another for what they receive. This, of course, is a simple error of transferring to the economist the frustration or anger that should be directed at the scarcities of the world. It is about as sensible as blam-ing the meteorologist for drought (or flood). And it may have been prompted by the witch-doctor pretensions of some economists to make rain by schemes for abolishing unemployment in a world of change, preventing inflation so long as the supply of money is con-trolled by politicians, achieving equality in a world of diverse human abilities, or annihilating poverty in a world of scarcity.

The truth is the opposite of the sociologists' complaint. To begin with the 'wicked motive' bogey: there is an obvious fallacy here. An argument is not wrong because interests indirectly or unintentionally benefit; probably all ideas benefit some interests. In any event, consequences matter more to people affected than motives. But more important: in his method of analysis, the economist who never loses sight of the realities underlying costs and prices, supply and demand, profit and loss does more good for people as individuals than the sociologist who discusses policy in terms of 'the pensioners', 'the sick', 'the disadvantaged'. The economist must analyse the benefits and the costs to *individuals*. The sociologist (Titmuss was the arch-exponent of this approach) is forever talking about *groups* – sometimes enormous like 'the pensioners' ($8\frac{1}{2}$ million) or 'Council tenants' (6 million), very large like 'hospital patients' (450,000) or 'deserted wives' (650,000), or less large like one-parent families with four or more children (about 50,000) – in all of which the individual person is submerged and out of sight.

Economists who believe that social policies must be built up on the subjective evaluations and judgements of individuals are more compassionate than sociologists who believe, sincerely or arrogantly, that they can judge what people 'need' by their physical, mental or legal characteristics ('old', 'sub-normal', 'deserted') which may have little to do with their income, circumstances, or requirements and therefore with their 'needs'.

In studying costs, the economist, moreover, is being more concerned about humanity than is the sociologist who sees the 'needs' of a group and calls for state action to satisfy them whatever the cost and *without reference to needs elsewhere of other groups*. Cost includes opportunity cost: no economist would advocate satisfying one set of needs in, say, housing unless the opportunities foregone showed that the resources called for could not be better used in health, pensions or elsewhere. It is the sociologist who is being callous when he calls for more help for this, that, or the other group without counting the cost. His motives do not help the deserving; his consequences harm them.

Helping the poor to pay

The second objection is more specific: people simply cannot affort to pay for education or any of the other services supplied by local and central government. How can the poor, or even the average earner, afford to pay school fees, doctors' bills, high rents, library charges, ambulance fares, refuse collection costs, water charges, full-cost parking charges, etc. etc? This objection seems to be decisive. Yet on examination it has very little substance.

In the first place, the very term 'cannot afford' is question-begging. Whatever our income, there is always something we cannot afford. But that means only we are spending our money on other things because we prefer them. The poor man who says he can't afford better shoes for his children means that he and his wife would rather buy more food for them. The middle-income man who says he can't afford a holiday means he would rather keep up his smoking or motoring. The rich man who says he can't afford a boat is saying he prefers a Rolls. No one can have enough of everything. We all 'cannot afford' something.

But do we in the 1970s really prefer the things on which we spend our money (or what is left after tax) to the things supplied for us by the politicians and officials who use our taxes? Do we really prefer spending on clothes, cars, cosmetics to spending on education, health and housing? Broadly our public services often seem shabby and scrimped in contrast to the private services, which are more to our taste and in which we take more pride. That is what the eloquent American phrase-maker Professor J.K. Galbraith meant when he popularised 'private affluence, public squalor'. But he misunderstood the reasons for the difference, and therefore drew the wrong conclusions for policy. He was condemning ordinary people for spending too much on their personal pleasures and individual indulgences and too little on the much more important public services. He therefore condemned commercial enterprise (run, of course, by the very same ordinary people) for pandering to their profligacies, and he condemned the very same ordinary people for not paying enough in taxes for better public services.

Like social reformers down the decades, he took the easy path of writing for a human species as yet unknown, not for the people of his day. Human nature can change, and may become more saintly in the future. But we must design institutions for man as he is now. 1977 man evidently prefers to spend his money himself than have it spent for him by others, whatever their pretence that they yearn to serve him. What he spends on himself is called private goods; what others spend it on is called public services. The commonsense conclusion – which Professor Galbraith did not see – is that we should let people spend more of their money themselves so that further squalor (in, say, education) is turned into private affluence (better schools) because they would spend more on education, etc. by diverting money from entertainment, etc. What matters is not who supplies the services or what they are called (public or private) but that they are supplied at all, that they suit us, and that they use our resources efficiently. There is no virtue in public services divorced from individual circumstances, preferences, even idiosyncrasies, at which superior people turn up their toffee noses.

In any event, if it is true that the income of 5, 10 or 15 per cent of the people is too low to pay charges because they have little or no expenditure to divert from entertainment, etc., it does not follow that the only way to provide them with public services is to supply the services free, both to them and to all the other 85, 90 or 95 per cent. The 5 to 15 per cent could be put in the same position as the 85 to 95 per cent by topping up their incomes with a reverse income tax.[88] They, too, could then be on the way to afford to pay.

Who pays now?

To say that the British cannot afford to pay for education, etc., is simply not true. Who else has paid for British public services except the British? It is only in the last few years that sheikhs and other rich creditors have lent us masses of money we could not earn for ourselves to enable us to keep our public services going: in the past the British were a nation of overseas lenders, not borrowers.

The British have *as a nation* long paid for their public services. In the past, the richest families helped to pay for the poorer (though the poor always paid for themselves through indirect taxes more than is usually recognised).

Today, the truth which no politician shouts from the roof-tops is that, except at the extremes of income, *the British family is increasingly paying for its own public services.* As we shall see, a very large part of the taxes paid by households is simply returned to them in a vast, wasteful shifting of coals to Newcastle. This little acknowledged but vitally important truth lies at the centre of the whole argument and we shall examine it in some detail.

Macro-taxes

First, let us grasp the huge macro-economic total of taxes. In 1974, to enable government to supply us with entirely or partly free goods of

TABLE D: TAX-AS-YOU-BUY

(1974; the figures are much higher now)

Purchase	Tax £million
Beer	592
Spirits	626
Wines, cider & perry	154
Tobacco	1,462
Clothing	376
Motor cars and cycles	231
Furniture & floor coverings	97
Chemists' goods	65
Recreational goods	113
Petrol and oil	852
Travel	72
Entertainment and recreation	59
Etc, etc.	

nearly £42 billion, income tax took £7 billion out of wages and salaries, not far short of £3 billion in tax on companies, £2¾ billion from employees and nearly £2 billion from employers in national insurance, and £3 billion in rates, and a lot of other taxes – surtax, taxes on capital, death duties, and others bringing in several billion more. In all, £11½ billion came from direct taxes on individuals, £10 billion from indirect taxes, and other taxes on companies; the rest was raised by borrowing.

We might then glance down the depressing list of taxes levied on purchases:

These indirect taxes are less obvious to the people who pay them than are direct assaults on the pay-slip in the form of PAYE, but even the direct taxes do not necessarily affect people in the way they think. There is an important distinction between where taxes initially land and where they finally end up: the difference between what economists call impact and incidence. Taxes imposed on industry, whether giant companies or self-employed one-man firms, on their purchases, sales, earnings or capital, may, if the demand for their products is strong (inelastic), be passed on to others – customers, suppliers or employees. So government does not know where such taxes end up. To this extent its taxation policies may be shooting wide of the mark and its claim to superior wisdom is empty. It taxes the baker on his petrol, but the tax may ultimately be paid by the pensioner or widow who buys the bread. So much for all-wise, all-knowing government and its scientific policies. In much of its financing it is almost as blind as a bat.

Micro-taxes

So total 'macro' tax figures are not sufficiently illuminating to the individual taxpayer. What is required is 'micro' information on taxes paid by individuals or families. Much more interesting – exciting or dismaying – than the total taxes are the official figures of taxes paid by each household, particularly whether it pays more in taxes than it receives in benefits, or less. Fortunately the government Central Statistical Office (CSO) has assembled such figures since the early 1960's,[121] though they are hardly known to ordinary people, for whom this book is primarily written.

The statistics have been based on a sample of households in which members aged 16 and over are asked by the Department of Employment for details of income (including government benefits in cash and kind), taxes paid, and purchases over 14 days (to assess taxes paid on them indirectly). The main purpose has been to yield information on expenditure to adjust the 'weights' in the index of retail prices. (Over the years there has been falling expenditure on bread and more on Scotch salmon, less on lard and more on butter, and so on). The number of households studied in 1974 was 6,695 – lower than usual because of the two General Elections in February and October. The information is collected for each household rather than for each family or individual person because all the occupants of a house or flat share, to some extent, in housing, fuel, lighting, food and perhaps other items, so it would be difficult to separate the taxes on pooled purchases of, or subsidies on, food, rent, rates, etc. paid or received by each family or individual.

The survey thus covered taxes paid by (or for) each household – taxes on income, national insurance contributions, taxes on purchases (cars and drink, VAT on other goods and services), local rates, and taxes on what are called 'intermediate products', such as local rates on industrial property and employers' national insurance contributions attributable to each household. These taxes (£21.42 billion) paid for just over half of the £41.61 billion of government expenditure. The other taxes that could not be attributed to separate households – mainly corporation tax and capital taxes – covered about 20 per cent of government expenditure. A further 13 per cent of expenditure was covered by trading income (rents, interests, etc.). The remaining 15 per cent was the gap between government expenditure and the revenue it raised in taxes, etc. (This is the measure of government over-spending, misleadingly called in official documents the public sector borrowing requirement (PSBR), which rather implies that the government can spend as much as it likes and simply plug the gap by borrowing.) The taxes not allocated to households were thus a little under 30 per cent.

Social benefits

On the government expenditure side the survey covered the services that the CSO officials said could be allocated to single households. Benefits in cash were obvious and easy. Subsidies on housing and food could be calculated from the information on expenditure supplied by each household. The benefits in kind – state education, the NHS, school meals, milk and welfare foods – could also be estimated as averages according to the number of children in the household and the average use of health services, etc. in the country as a whole. In all, the allocated benefits accounted for $37\frac{1}{2}$ per cent of total government expenditure, or £15.62 out of £41.61 billion expenditure. In this sense, we may note, these public services are officially acknowledged as providing *private* benefits rather than being public goods proper. Moreover, only the *cost* of the benefits could be allocated, and these, the survey admits, 'may bear little relation to the value which the household would itself put on these services'. In short the official document was saying that where there are no charges freely paid by users there is ignorance. Government costs ('inputs') are not necessarily indicators of value ('outputs').

Other government services, said the officials, were not allocated. Here we are in the thick of the argument of this book. First, defence (the archetypal public good and the largest single item, 12 per cent of government expenditure including external relations) and tax collection and other administrative costs 'are not generally thought of as conferring benefits of a kind which can be allocated to individual households'. The officials could hardly be expected to add that if public services were financed by pricing as *much* as possible (not as *little* as convenient for politicians and public officials not anxious to see their domain diminished), tax collection and administrative costs would be much smaller.

Then again, expenditure on regional support and industrial development, such as investment grants, research and roads (about $8\frac{1}{2}$ per cent), was not allocated to households because, said the officials, although they influence the general weight of taxation as well as jobs and therefore incomes, 'there is, at least at present, no practical way of estimating these effects on individual households'.[121] But there is a way of calculating the personal benefit from roads (by the black box for long-distance roads, Chapter 8); and the economic argument for regional policy is very shaky[118] and much of this expenditure should not have been incurred at all.

What are misleadingly called 'environmental and protective services' – refuse collection, museums, libraries, parks, fire services, police, water, sewage, etc. (8.9 per cent) – were also not allocated because, continued the officials, 'not enough is known about the extent to which each is used' (by each household). This is precisely, as argued in Chapters 7 and 8, the group of local government services in which a large element of pricing could be introduced; and it would make plain the extent of private benefit, not only to each household, but also for each family and even each individual.

Finally, capital expenditure on the social services and public corporations was also not allocated (11.6 per cent). Households derive current benefits from past capital expenditure on schools, hospitals, etc., 'but to value them', persisted the officials, 'requires more information than is presently available'. Here again, pricing, facilitated by the new dimension of choice conveyed by education, health and housing vouchers, could identify the personal family and household benefit (Chapters 4, 5 and 6). These unallocated benefits in the Family Expenditure Surveys accounted in 1974 for $62\frac{1}{2}$ per cent of all government expenditure, yet a large part of them are private benefits.

A final comment on the official (or, at least, these officials'[12]) opinion, half true and half false: 'If this analysis were trying to estimate [the] effects [of allocated expenditure such as education and medical care] on the welfare of households, they should perhaps be measured in terms of the values placed upon them by the households themselves.' This is fundamentally true: only the user of a service can in the end know its value for him. Economists who hold this view have long adhered to the subjective theory of value, which derives from the Austrian school of economists, and which Professor (Lord) Robbins once explained graphically as 'nothing is valuable but thinking makes it so'. Unfortunately the official judgement concluded that there was 'no practicable way' of measuring the values placed on services by households. This is not true: there certainly is such a way, and there is no insuperable technical obstacle to measurement. The only obstacles are intellectual confusion, political conservatism, civil service obstruction, and trade union defence of vested interests. The way is charging.

Each kind of household's loss or gain

The important question is: what was the net effect on each household of this industrious governmental activity in moving money out of households in taxes and shifting benefits back in cash (insurance benefits, family allowances, pensions, etc.) and in kind (education, health and other services)? Who gains or loses in this vast game of swings and roundabouts?

To illustrate the net result, figures for eight families varying in size and income are shown in Table E(ii) with the detail of each main tax and benefit for the year 1974. Not surprisingly, since benefits often go to individuals rather than the family as a unit (family allowances and education for each child), the larger households received higher value in benefits than smaller households. So, within each income group, households with two adults and three children or three adults and four children received more in benefits than a household with two adults and two children. What is more surprising is that a wide range of households of middling size and income ended not much better off if their original income was relatively low, and not much worse off if their original income was relatively high. (Later figures will show much the same result.)

Table E(i) shows the gains and losses for each of the ten groups analysed by size of household. On balance only the sole adult and the household with four children gain; all the other groups lose. But the gains and losses are mostly within 20 per cent of original income. And in total, all groups together 'lose' 10 per cent of original income, of which a large part is the cost of erecting and running the swings and

TABLE E: THE SWINGS AND ROUNDABOUTS, 1974

(i) Total original and final income after paying taxes and adding benefits for 10 groups of household by size

Households		Average Income (£)		Result	
Size	Number	Original	Final	Gain (%)	Loss (%)
1 adult	1,255	931	1,103	18	—
2 adults	2,113	2,479	2,100	—	15
2 adults, 1 child	607	3,097	2,455	—	21
2 adults, 2 children	808	3,293	2,857	—	13
2 adults, 3 children	334	3,385	3,296	—	3
2 adults, 4 children	117	3,275	3,700	13	—
3 adults	510	3,914	3,052	—	22
3 adults, 1 child	199	4,216	3,686	—	13
3 adults, 2 children	116	3,844	3,723	—	3
4 adults	153	5,342	4,324	—	19
All households in sample	6,212	2,719	2,448	—	10

TABLE E:
THE SWINGS AND ROUNDABOUTS, 1974 — continued

(ii) Average original income and final income (£ per year) after paying all taxes and adding all benefits for eight types of household

	Retired	Non-retired	Retired and non-retired					
	1 adult	2 adults 0 children	2 adults 1 child	2 adults 2 children	2 adults 2 children	2 adults 3 children	2 adults 3 children	2 adults 1 child
Number of households	579	229	74	76	118	64	64	26
Original income range	under 381	3099–3749	1749–2115	1749–2115	2116–2560	2561–3098	3099–3749	over 5490
average	88	3403	1960	1957	2366	2829	3399	8943
Add benefits								
(i) direct in cash								
family allowance	–	–	–	45	45	98	99	–
retirement & old age pension	444	36	–	–	–	–	–	–
widow's pension	14	13	21	–	–	–	–	–
disablement and war disability pension	8	1	5	–	3	–	–	–
invalidity pension & allowance	4	1	10	21	2	–	–	–
unemployment benefit	–	5	4	7	6	–	–	–
sickness & industrial injury benefit	–	13	27	13	11	22	5	–
family income supplement	–	–	–	1	–	3	5	–
supplementary benefit	116	1	19	7	10	–	–	–
maternity benefit	–	1	–	–	6	2	3	–
death grant	1	–	–	–	–	–	1	4
redundancy payment	–	1	–	–	1	–	–	–
other cash benefits	3	–	–	–	–	–	–	–
(ii) indirect (subsidies)								
housing	73	43	44	61	34	78	37	12
food	9	16	20	25	27	34	34	21

	Retired	Non-retired			Retired and non-retired			
	1 adult	2 adults 0 children	2 adults 1 child	2 adults 2 children	2 adults 2 children	2 adults 3 children	2 adults 3 children	2 adults 1 child
(iii) direct in kind								
education	–	15	96	268	308	561	570	137
NHS	108	110	209	191	189	192	201	139
welfare foods	–	–	6	19	14	27	34	7
Total benefits	780	256	461	658	656	1017	989	322
Original income plus all benefits	868	3659	2421	2615	3022	3846	4388	9265
Deduct taxes								
(i) direct								
income tax and surtax	3	561	195	150	229	320	364	2145
NI contributions (employees')	–	154	98	99	117	135	144	172
(ii) indirect								
local rates	48	80	60	66	67	78	83	135
on purchases[1]	43	381	264	273	301	321	407	603
on other items[2]	30	128	96	97	115	130	138	274
Total taxes	124	1304	713	685	829	984	1136	3329
Final income	744	2356	1708	1930	2194	2862	3251	5936
Net result of all taxes and benefits	+656	–1047	–254	–27	–172	+32	–148	–3007

Source: Abstracted from Table 3, *Economic Trends*, Government Statistical Service, HMSO, February, 1976

1 Customs and Excise duties on beer, wines, spirits, tobacco, oil, betting, etc.; VAT; motor vehicle duties; driving licences, television licences, stamp duties.
2 These are rates and taxes on goods and services used in the production of goods and services bought by consumers. They include local rates on commercial and industry property, vehicle licences, customs and excise duties on hydrocarbon oils, import duties, stamp duties, employers' NI, NHS and redundancy contributions.
(*Note*: totals may not add up to the sum of items because individual figures are estimated to nearest whole numbers.)

roundabouts. Personal incomes in 1974 were £75 billion, so the running costs of the tax/benefits game may be up to £7½ billion.

The figures for each group of households within a given income and size are not as reliable as the figures for the sample as a whole. So the smaller the size- or income-group the less useful the averages and estimates that emerged. It is convenient to show the figures in tabular form, but the argument can be followed in words here. Readers will find it instructive to keep a record of their own household figures for a fortnight and compare them with the average for their range of income and size (kind) of household. They will teach you a lot you did not know about the half (on average) of your income you have not thought about much because it is spent for you by others.

These figures are the best available statistics for measuring taxes and benefits. In spite of their incompleteness and limitations [76] the figures are used by the government statisticians to give 'a comprehensible picture of the impact of government expenditure and taxation on individual households in different circumstances'. [121] What emerges is evidence that the 'can't afford' argument is very suspect. The figures suggest massive movements of tax-money (half of income on average, much more in many households) out of homes in Wapping, Worcester, Wolverhampton and Wigtown to Whitehall and town-hall, passing a massive opposite movement of money (family allowances, etc.) and services from Whitehall or town-hall to Wapping, Worcester, Wolverhampton and Wigtown.

This intriguing dénouement which, to repeat, few politicians mention, still less emphasise, raises the fascinating question: 'If large numbers of us are paying for our own benefits, more or less, why do we have them controlled by people in government offices? Why can't we buy them ourselves?'

Billions of taxes are returned

The more the edifice of taxes and benefits is examined the more it shows that we have all evidently been the victims of a political hoax (which would long ago have been denounced as an obscene swindle if it had been the work of 'the capitalists'). For it shows that, when governments say that they must supply this, that or the other because we the people 'cannot afford' to pay for them ourselves, *it is they who have made us incapable of paying*. This confidence trick has gone back over a century (Professor West showed it was true of working people and their indirect taxes in the 1870s and earlier[116, 117]) but we have only in recent years had the figures to show how wide-ranging it is in our day.

Take the first of the eight kinds of households (Table Eii): the retired person living alone (probably a widow whose husband died a few years after he retired). Such households in the sample had an original income (perhaps from the husband's occupational, trade union or other pension or her small earnings) of £88 on average. The retirement pension, supplementary benefit and benefits in kind yielded £780. Total £868. Even at this low standard of living, rates and indirect taxes reduced the final income to £744. But at least the mighty machinery of benefit and taxes raised income from a derisory £88 (average) to £744.

At the other income extreme of the eight households the largest original income recorded was a group with over £5,490 a year. Here there were too few households with two adults and one child for very close calculations. Their average income was £8,943. They received only £6 in cash benefits but £316 in benefits in kind (untaxed and therefore worth much more: I argued some years ago[106] that they should be taxed) raising their gross figure to £9,265. This was reduced by £3,329 paid in taxes, mostly income tax. The final net income of £5,936 was thus £3,007 less than the original average income for the group. The mighty machine of taxes and benefits had redistributed income away from the upper end of the income range.

The extremes of family size are also affected by the tax-benefit machine. The household in the more or less middling income group of £3,099 to £3,749 with an average of £3,403 was left substantially worse off. Such households in the sample had no children under 18 (perhaps because couples could not have children, or where the children had married). They received £256 in benefits but paid £1,304 in taxes, ending £1,047 worse off at £2,356. Whether you regard it as redistributing income (though such households are hardly rich) or as taking from childless couples or from parents who had brought up a family, again the massive machine had worked.

But what of the typical family households in the middle, with more or less average incomes and numbers of children? Apart from the extremes of income, and in families with two or three children, the tax-benefit machine left much less of a mark. Households of two adults and two children in the income range £1,749 to £2,115, an average of

£1,957 a year, much less than the national average, received £658 in benefits but paid out £685 in taxes. Their final income was thus £27 less than they started with. A lot of activity for a little result: a third of income taken in taxes, and put back in benefits, less a slice for the officials who assess and collect taxes, return benefits in cash and run benefits in kind. Net result: final income down by 1.38 per cent. And against this they lose influence over the £478 of benefits in kind.

Households of the same size but with rather more income (an average of £2,366) ended up £172 worse off than they started after receiving £656 in benefits and paying £831 in taxes. Shifting 28 per cent of their income in and 35 per cent out left them 7.27 per cent worse off.

Or take two rather larger types of household: two adults and three children in the income range £2,561 to £3,098. They had an average original income of £2,829. After a lot of heaving and shoving, with £1,017 in benefits and £984 in taxes, they finished £32 better off. Again a mouse (plus 1.13 per cent) out of a mountain (a third in and out).

In the higher income range of £3,099 to £3,749, households with an average original income of £3,399 ended £148 worse off (4.35 per cent) after receiving £989 in benefits and paying £1,136 in taxes (again around a third in and out).

Finally, households of two adults and one child in the income range £1,749 to £2,115 – markedly less than the national wage – started with an average of £1,960, received £461 in benefits, paid out a surprising £713 in taxes and ended £254 worse off. More than a third was moved out, less than a third was moved back: result, the household was left 12.96 per cent worse off. (It lost more because of its small size than it gained because of its low income.)

Two main conclusions follow. The first is that all this activity in raising taxes and returning benefits seems to have only a balancing effect in altering the final distribution of income in most households. There must be a better way of arranging this relatively small amount of true redistribution without heaving and shoving such vast amounts of taxes and benefits to and fro. Many more households would then no longer be 'too poor to pay', and the excuse for providing 'free' services would have evaporated. They could be made customers who paid charges for choice.

The second is that the persistence with raising taxes to finance the increasing element of private benefit in public services is driving taxes further down the income scale. Households with barely average incomes are being taxed, and even those receiving state benefits have to pay part of them back. This is not only coals to Newcastle; if the official figures are about right, it looks more like a vicious circle of benefits in Bedlam. The state treats its citizens as intelligent enough to elect legislators, competent enough to live daily lives without poisoning or killing themselves; yet, in thus depriving them of the power to dispose of their incomes, it questions their humanity, their competence, their responsibility and integrity. It mocks their intelligence most by telling millions they are too poor to pay when it is the state itself that makes many of them poor.

How much taxation is 'abortive'?

How far is the state itself, by taxation, making people unable to pay for its benefits? How much British taxation is 'abortive' in the sense that it could be left with taxpayers to enable them to pay in the first place? How much goes back in cash or kind *to the very same households whence it came*?

In the USA, Professor Friedman has estimated that only about a third of the billions of dollars spent on social benefits in the mid-1960s was required to make the lowest incomes up to the minimum income regarded as the poverty line so that poverty in this sense was wiped out. Two thirds, it would seem, need not have been raised for this redistributive purpose and was 'abortive'.

The British statistics do not make this calculation. Yet it is one of the most important that could have emerged from them, even if the benefits statistics account for only three eighths of government expenditure and taxes allocated cover only rather over half of government expenditure. Moreover, what is important for individual decision-making is not the total macro-figure for the country as a whole but the micro-finances of each family or household. The figures for each of the 6,695 households in the sample are not available, but I have calculated them for the 6,051 in each of the 69 groups large enough for separate figures to be available (those with over 10 in each group). This is a first rough approximation because the figures were averages for each group. The results are shown in Table F.

The 6,051 households paid just over £7 million in taxes and received rather over £3¼ million in benefits (the totals of the last two

TABLE F: ABORTIVE TAXATION, OR COALS TO NEWCASTLE

a first approximation by averages for groups of households, 1974

| Households | | Original income (£) | Average for each group of households | | | | Total taxes | |
Composition	number		taxes paid £	benefits received £	taxes returned in benefits £	%	paid	returned
1 adult (retired)	579	under 381	125	781	125	100	72,375	72,375
	46	381 — 556	183	633	183	100	8,418	8,418
	38	557 — 815	286	631	286	100	10,868	10,868
	27	816 — 1,193	424	553	424	100	11,448	11,448
	20	1,194 — 1,748	542	635	542	100	10,840	10,840
	14	749 — 2,560	781	578	578	74	10,934	8,092
2 adults (retired)	340	under 381	225	1,241	225	100	76,500.	76,500
	73	301 — 556	242	1,090	242	100	17,666	17,666
	56	557 — 815	370	1,045	370	100	20,720	20,720
	46	816 — 1,193	493	1,034	493	100	22,678	22,678
	31	1,194 — 1,748	661	1,024	661	100	20,491	20,491
	30	1,749 — 2,560	793	872	793	100	23,790	23,790
	18	2,561 — 3,749	1,293	928	928	72	23,274	16,704

| Households | | Original income (£) | Average for each group of households | | | | Total taxes | |
Composition	number		taxes paid £	benefits received £	taxes returned in benefits £	taxes returned in benefits %	paid	returned
1 adult (not retired)	69	under 381	155	969	155	100	10,695	10,695
	19	381 – 556	223	650	223	100	4,237	4,237
	43	557 – 815	310	561	310	100	13,330	13,330
	63	816 – 1,193	400	413	400	100	25,200	25,200
	107	1,194 – 1,748	605	290	290	48	64,735	31,030
	118	1,749 – 2,560	863	147	147	17	101,834	17,346
	63	2,561 – 3,749	1,146	130	130	11	72,198	8,190
	29	3,750 – 5,489	1,747	79	79	4.5	50,663	2,291
	12	5,490 +	3,116	95	95	3.0	37,392	1,140
2 adults (not retired)	27	under 381	309	1,105	309	100	8,343	8,343
	18	381 – 556	290	1,171	290	100	5,220	5,220
	42	557 – 815	310	983	310	100	13,020	13,020
	57	816 – 1,193	429	906	429	100	24,453	24,453
	138	1,194 – 1,748	583	551	551	95	80,454	76,038
	318	1,749 – 2,560	837	378	378	45	266,166	120,204
	445	2,561 – 3,749	1,184	292	292	25	526,880	129,940
	339	3,750 – 5,489	1,647	197	197	12	558,333	66,783
	120	5,490 +	2,789	197	197	7	334,680	23,640

| Households | | Original income (£) | Average for each group of households | | | | Total taxes | |
Composition	number		taxes paid £	benefits received £	taxes returned in benefits £	%	paid	returned
2 adults 1 child	11	816 — 1,193	332	1,000	332	100	3,652	3,652
	45	1,194 — 1,748	561	631	561	100	25,245	25,245
	177	1,749 — 2,560	784	461	461	59	138,768	81,597
	221	2,561 — 3,749	1,112	436	436	39	245,752	96,356
	114	3,750 — 5,489	1,550	388	388	25	176,700	44,232
	26	5,490 +	3,330	322	322	10	86,580	8,372
2 adults 2 children	49	1,194 — 1,748	540	871	540	100	26,460	26,460
	194	1,749 — 2,560	773	657	657	85	149,962	127,458
	320	2,561 — 3,749	1,071	641	641	60	342,720	205,120
	173	3,750 — 5,489	1,475	652	652	44	255,175	112,796
	51	5,490 +	2,403	646	646	27	122,553	32,946
2 adults 3 children	12	under 381	430	2,320	430	100	5,160	5,160
	21	1,194 — 1,748	465	1,201	465	100	9,765	9,765
	63	1,749 — 2,560	746	983	746	100	46,998	46,998
	128	2,561 — 3,749	1,060	1,002	1,002	95	135,680	128,256
	70	3,750 — 5,489	1,406	1,009	1,009	72	98,420	70,630
	34	5,490 +	2,499	853	853	34	84,966	29,002
2 adults 4 children	17	1,194 — 1,748	453	1,593	453	100	7,701	7,701
	26	1,749 — 2,560	663	1,459	663	100	17,238	17,238
	31	2,561 — 3,749	1,035	1,379	1,035	100	32,085	32,085
	26	3,750 — 5,489	1,406	1,313	1,313	93	36,556	34,138
	10	5,490 +	2,493	1,253	1,253	50	24,930	12,530

TABLE F: ABORTIVE TAXATION, OR COALS TO NEWCASTLE
a first approximation by averages for groups of households, 1974

| Households | | Original income (£) | Average for each group of households | | | | Total taxes | |
Composition	number		taxes paid £	benefits received £	taxes returned in benefits £	%	paid	returned
3 adults	10	under 381	407	1,631	407	100	4,070	4,070
	19	1,446 – 1,748	716	1,104	716	100	13,604	13,604
	61	1,749 – 2,560	1,820	2,149	1,820	100	111,020	111,020
	141	2,561 – 3,749	2,503	1,306	1,306	52	352,923	184,146
	166	3,750 – 5,489	3,544	969	969	27	588,304	160,854
	83	5,490 +	2,761	421	421	15	229,163	34,943
3 adults 1 child	18	2,116 – 2,560	841	1,012	841	100	15,138	15,138
	54	2,561 – 3,749	2,259	1,791	1,791	79	121,986	96,714
	69	3,750 – 5,489	3,188	1,744	1,744	55	219,972	120,336
	36	5,490 +	2,677	876	876	33	96,372	31,536
3 adults 2 children	41	2,561 – 3,749	2,085	2,663	2,085	100	85,485	85,485
	41	3,750 – 5,489	3,134	2,259	2,259	72	128,494	92,619
	16	5,490 +	2,308	1,122	1,122	49	36,928	17,952
4 adults	20	3,099 – 3,749	1,298	1,794	1,298	100	25,960	25,960
	51	3,750 – 5,489	3,381	1,633	1,633	48	172,431	83,283
	61	5,490 +	2,703	693	693	26	164,883	42,273

Source: abstracted and calculated from 121, References, p.220.

columns). In all therefore 46 per cent, or not far short of half, of the taxes were refunded in benefits *to the very same households*. This calculation applies only to the taxes that could be traced to households. We do not know how much of the taxes not analysed by the government statisticians were eventually returned to the households from which they came. I would expect that probably much more than half and possibly as much as two thirds or three quarters of all British taxes are raised unnecessarily and wastefully in this way. This is a measure of the enormous sums that could be left with people to use, or to learn to use in time, to buy goods and services now supplied by government.

The figures available provide, at least, the most reasonably reliable figures measuring the swings and roundabouts of taxes and benefits. As pricing is spread to other benefits, and it becomes possible to trace other taxes to households, we shall be able to make a more complete assessment of the extent of abortive taxation and unnecessary government. This in itself is a powerful case for charging to yield the *information* we cannot collect in any other way for government policy to make sense because it would then be based on knowledge rather than politicised judgement or guess-work.

The figures have been calculated to show the average taxes paid by households in each of the 69 groups and the average value of the benefits they received. It is then possible to calculate the percentages of taxes returned by the state in benefits. Where taxes were less than benefits, all the taxes, 100 per cent, can be regarded as being returned; where taxes exceed benefits, less than 100 per cent. Thus, in the 1974 households of a sole adult, the group with original income up to £1,748 had, on average, all their taxes returned. The groups with the highest income, £1,749 to £2,560 (there were some with higher income but too few to yield averages), paid more in taxes than they received in benefits, which were 74 per cent of their taxes. Within each group, household figures would have varied because of differences in expenditure (and therefore indirect taxes), tax allowance (for dependents, life assurance, mortgage interest) and so on.

Of the 6,051 households, 2,068, or over a third, had all their taxes returned in benefits, and could possibly not have been taxed at all (subject to the qualifications below). A further 486 households had 80 to 99 per cent returned; 517 had 60 to 79 per cent returned; 1,062 had 40 to 59 per cent; and the remainder, 1,918, had less than 40 per cent.

They could all therefore have been taxed either very little or much less than they were, and some – those with the lowest incomes or most children – almost not at all.

How much, in money, of taxes could be left with families – or not levied in the first place? The calculations suggest that, on average, that is for all families in the country as a whole, the proportion of taxes that are now levied to pay for 'the social wage' but that could be left with families is not less than half. I have argued that it is probably higher. But even at half it would mean that, with 'the social wage' around £1,000, families could be left with an average of about £500 a year to spend as they, rather than the politicians or officials, thought best. There would be some possible general requirements, such as health insurance to cover major medical risks and minimum educational standards; but even here families would have a choice of health insurer not confined to the state, and a choice of educational method not confined to state schools. There would be no need for compulsory school attendance at all, and certainly not a fixed minimum age for all children whatever their abilities or potentialities. And families would, of course, be able to take advice on how to spend their money from a wide range of advisers, public and private, official, charitable, secular, spiritual, voluntary or commercial.

Interest attaches not only to the number of households that might not be taxed at all, or not very much, but also to their income. For they are the poorest, or the near-poor – precisely those that advocates of compulsory government services say are least able to pay for services. Even retired couples (two adults) with original incomes up to £1,748 and receiving around £1,000 in benefits paid several hundred pounds in taxes.

What happens if we omit the 'rich' and examine the effect on the others? The income group with £5,490 and over totals 449 households, or 7 per cent of the sample. If we take them as a fair approximation to 'the rich', we are left arguing that the remainder, 93 per cent of households, must be supplied with free (or subsidised) services because they are too 'poor' to pay. But the official statistics show that, except for 2,068 households with the lower incomes, the 'poor' people pay *more* in taxes than they receive in benefits. The 2,068 form only 34 per cent of the households. So 59 per cent (93 per cent less 34 per cent) of households are *made* 'poor' by the very state that says it must tax them to supply 'free' services they are too poor to buy. 59 per cent of all households in the UK is over 10½ million – or, say, around 35 million people. So much for the poverty argument that the British people cannot pay for the private benefits in public services.

It must now be clear that there is enormous scope for leaving families with much or most of their taxes. And it must also be accepted that the 'poverty' excuse for supplying them with free services is, for not far short of two-thirds of families, circular reasoning: their original (gross) incomes are high enough to pay if they were not taxed in the first place, or not as much as they are now.

What about the poor who receive more in benefits than they pay in taxes? They can be helped to pay in two ways: mainly by reverse taxes; possibly also by lower expenditure taxes on the sort of goods they tend to buy. Thus by reverse taxes for the real poor (with lower incomes) and returned (or rather abolished) taxes for the artificially state-created 'poor', *all* could be made equal in status, dignity and consumer authority over the services they use. And they could all have the bonus of an enormous reduction in the bureaucracy and more efficient government with more attention to real public goods that are now neglected because of lack of tax funds.

These calculations must be regarded only as a first approximation because ideally they should be made for each household separately rather than for the groups; the figures given by the households in the sample cannot all be checked; and they may not strictly represent payments in and out during a single year. But they are the best figures we have. Let the government therefore do the more complete and refined calculations to provide a Twentieth Century Domesday Book from which each family can tell where it stands. We shall then know the full extent of abortive taxation. And until that day let the 'poverty' argument for free public services be abandoned as based on lack of knowledge or on special pleading unsupported by reasoning, statistics or common sense.

Are the British irresponsible?

The third objection to charging is that some people who could pay would not pay. They would be short-sighted, inhuman, callous, self-indulgent, brutal. They would live in hovels, not send their children to school, not insure against ill-health, not have their refuse or sewage removed; mothers and fathers would abandon their young children while at work; they would not pay for water; their lives would be nasty, brutish, and probably short.

To list the spine-chilling examples is to show how unreal they are. I do not recognise, in this picture, the British in the second half of the twentieth century, regarded by visitors as the most considerate, helpful, tolerant and civilised people in the world, especially to strangers. There are some such people in every country: in the richest as well as the poorest; in Britain, in the United States, as well as in India and Russia. How many there are in Britain we do not know – 2 per cent? 5 per cent? Advocates of state paternalism insist there would be many if people were left to themselves, and that those who are not must be treated as if they are until there are none.

How far we should run people's lives is itself a central question. People do not have to join in a free society with the burden of making choices in markets; they may drop out. Even where it may be desirable to prevent foolish or selfish people from neglecting themselves or their children, it is by no means clear that free government services are the best way. That method has been tried in Britain for a century without making everyone more responsible. It may, indeed, have the opposite effect: some people will not learn to take care of themselves – or their children – if they are taken care of by others. If social policy had been less paternalistic, years of practice in day-to-day responsibility would have taught more to be responsible. Yet in the name of equality it is argued by paternalists, more on the Left than on the Right, that social policies and government services should treat everyone alike so that the exceptional should not feel singled out or isolated. So if 5 per cent are irresponsible, the 95 per cent responsible must be treated as irresponsible. This is the argument that has maintained taxes at the high and rising levels to pay for services that more and more people could be buying for themselves.

Would charging destroy welfare?

The supporters of this irresponsible argument tend to claim that charging would create havoc by destroying the fabric of social services built up over a century. This argument is defective.

First, initially the charges are to be for services provided by government. If government can induce citizens to pay their taxes, increasingly against their inclinations, it can induce them to pay charges that will show them what they are paying for. There are apparent differences. In favour of taxes, paradoxically, is the lack of knowledge of tax-prices: knowing prices through charges may cause users to hesitate or wish to rebel when they know for the first time what services like education or fire-fighting cost. In favour of charges is this very knowledge, which might encourage users to pay more readily by economising elsewhere. But since government services are supplied for all citizens whether they pay for them by taxes or charges, the objection does not apply. Children will still be required to be educated, although not necessarily in state schools. Health insurance, not necessarily for all costs and risks but for major risks or catastrophic costs, could still be made obligatory, as is third party motor insurance, though not necessarily with the government.

Second, the case for compulsion can hardly continue for ever. Fewer husbands would neglect their wives' health, or parents their children's health or education, or families their homes, than did so twenty-five, fifty or seventy-five years ago. If there are more, there must be something alarmingly wrong with government control of education and the social and moral environment it has built up over a century since 1870.

Third, if there is a minority, whether growing or declining, that refuses to pay for a service considered desirable for all to use, the argument for forcing them to use it by making them pay in taxes supposes that they are less likely to use it if they pay by charges. The opposite seems the more likely. People will make the most of a service if they know they are paying for it and know how much it costs, because they then appreciate what a sacrifice they are making of other things. State school parents have no idea of school costs. Fee-paying parents know it is more or less £250 a term in day schools. Truancy would be less common if parents paid school fees through cash or vouchers; it is less common in private than in state schools. And much the same attitude would appear elsewhere: 'I am paying for this school (hospital, etc.) so I must make the best of it.'

The unacceptable cost of exclusive tax-paid services

There is a more fundamental objection to all-embracing compulsion by taxation. *If the price of all-embracing participation in a service is that no other method of payment for a possible alternative can be allowed, the price – in sacrifice of services unknown – is too high to pay.* It is probably true that the comprehensive method of secondary education cannot be judged unless all children in the catchment area are channelled into it by suppressing all other methods. That is a logically defensible proposition. But it is not one that can be accepted by anyone in a civilised society. Its implications are fearful. This approach to policy could be catastrophic, for it requires that all other methods should be suppressed. The case, at best, is for temporary closure of other schools in the area until the comprehensive method is tested. This argument is seductive but must be rejected. In practice forces of inertia working for continuance of the comprehensive method, even if it was seen to fail (in education, health or anywhere else), would be all the stronger once the other methods that could draw off dissatisfied parents were not available.

The case for universalising a technique by suppressing existing or potential alternatives is defective because it overlooks the unknown and untold externality of improvement by experimentation and innovation that has sustained the progress of civilised life. It blocks the development of new and better techniques.

The case for making all pay for a universal, comprehensive, exclusive, 'totalitarian' government service by taxes, because some would not pay charges or would try alternatives elsewhere, is similarly defective by circular reasoning. The apparently perfectionist technique is fatally *imperfect* because it requires suppression of alternatives – the only source of evidence by which its perfection can be proved.

Are the British gullible?

A fourth social objection to charging is that if it led some users to change between government suppliers (by moving between local authority areas) or from government to private suppliers, the chance of acquiring users would induce suppliers to attract them against their best interests.

The large unstated assumption is that users now receive the best possible services from their present government suppliers. Discussion of this aspect of government service is surprisingly naive in Britain, and much less sophisticated than in the USA. Perhaps complaints in recent years against the Post Office for its tardy letter post and inattentive telephone services, against unprompt government railways and road transport, indifferent quality of coal service, undependable refuse collection, inadequate police protection or corrupt council building may have made the British public more critical. But there is still a lingering, though lately evaporating, faith in civil servants as sea-green incorruptibles, still a trust in British 'public' men and officials, still a belief that any organisation described as 'public' must be 'in the public interest'.

This attitude is surprising from the British mixture of common sense, humour and capacity to see through pretence. A man is not made a public benefactor by being made a public official. It is still the truest working assumptions that family man will maximise his private satisfactions, business man his private profit, official man his official influence, and political man his political power. What they do with their profit, influence or power is their affair: they can use it selfishly or unselfishly according to how they are taught by family, school, or church. But much more understanding of public and political life is obtained by working from these realistic assumptions than by supposing that public men or government employees from town hall housing managers to Whitehall mandarins yearn to dispense nectar to all and sundry with never a thought for themselves or their families or concerns. American economists are ahead of British universities in their development of theories of public choice, democracy and politics,[8 to 12, 50] although they are being closely followed.[81, 100] There is no reason to suppose that government monopolies will safeguard their users better than suppliers (government or private) that have to satisfy their customers or lose them to competitors.

The objection that users will be at the mercy of persuasive suppliers is in any event at variance with the reaction of British consumers who *pay* for what they buy. If there is little prospect of alternative supply, as in wartime or local monopoly, they accept with good-humoured resignation what is offered. But if there are alternatives they are not supine or subservient: they expect good value or go elsewhere. The emergent wage-earner – and his wife – faced with the profusion of post-war labour-saving or leisure-serving products soon learned how to buy wisely. It is precisely in the 'public' services supplied by government that they have been inured to passive acceptance because their faculties of judgement and discrimination have atrophied, because they have never, or at best rarely, been exercised. The demanding customer at the pub, butcher, hairdresser or airport often becomes a subdued supplicant in the state headmaster's study, the matron's ward or the Council housing manager's office; the minority who become

aggressive to over-compensate for lack of bargaining power, demanding more than their due, distort the distribution. The result is arbitrary, the outcome of chance, not justice or 'fairness'.

What makes for social divisiveness?

A fifth objection to charging is that joint or collective payment by taxes for services shared by all without question of individual payment
has the unique quality of creating a sense of social cohesion that unites
everyone in the community. A public service that we use without payment makes us all feel at one with another. Something for which we
pay separately divides us from our fellow beings. This sense of community, or fellowship, underlies the best of utopian Socialist teaching
about men as brothers. It is also reflected in the Conservative feeling
that, however the British may differ, they are basically members of
One Nation. (The phrase was formulated to dramatise the contrast
with the Conservative Benjamin Disraeli's characterisation of the
nineteenth century British as Two Nations, the rich and the poor.) The
importance of the public services in creating or strengthening the sense
of social cohesion has been a repeated refrain in sociological writing
since the war.

If this anxiety about social cohesion is to be urged against individual payment, it should be examined more closely. Charging
would yield revenue for 'public' services that government has not been
able to raise in taxes. If 'public' services strengthen social cohesion, as
they may if they are *public* goods, charging is the only method
available when other methods of financing them are exhausted
because the limits of acceptable taxation have been reached.

If it is replied that charging may lead some people to prefer private
services (which it might) that is a risk that the defenders of 'public' services must take. The alternative is to extract still higher taxation from
reluctant taxpayers by enforcement that becomes increasingly more
stringent as the willing acceptance of taxation decreases and taxpayers
resort increasingly to avoidance and evasion. Increasingly stringent
enforcement can logically be argued by tax collectors, but it is hardly
likely to create or promote the social cohesion between lawmakers and
citizens, tax-gatherers and tax-payers desired by the supporters of
government expenditure. The dilemma is insoluble.

There is an even more fundamental doubt about the theory of social
cohesion through public services. The theory is that shared public ser-

vices create a sense of community. Each member of society says: 'This train/coal mine/generating station/rubbish dump/library/telephone kiosk/beach/abattoir is owned in common by all my fellow citizens and me. I own part of it. It binds them to me, and me to them. I will therefore take care of it.'

A noble conception. Or do we say: 'They tell me this is mine, but it is also everybody else's. Only a tiny part of it is mine, so small I can hardly imagine it. And whatever my tiny nominal ownership I have no say in the way it is used, no real control over it at all. It is not really mine; it is theirs. And, no matter how much care I take, it will do me no good if everyone else does not.'

Public services, especially as paying for them by taxes is increasingly resented, are seen not as everyone's property that all will protect and cherish, but as no one's property that is fair game for selfish use, abuse and exploitation. If each man's nominal ownership is tiny, public property is seen by each individual as owned by everyone else: the vast amorphous, anonymous 'Them' that has become the description of the unknown outsiders with no names or recognisable faces who in the real world seem collectively to control the public property that only in theory, in political tracts, on paper, in General Election manifestoes and speeches, belongs to everyman. It may be a bitter pill for the hopeful, generous-hearted advocates of public property who, for a century since the Fabians of the 1880s, have believed that all would own and share in mutual brotherly consideration. The truth is that ownership that is not individual, or possibly in very small groups, is ineffective. The environment is exploited, over-used, abused, ravaged and polluted because no one owns it. On paper it belongs to all of us, but in practice to none of us, so no one takes care of it, no one has an interest in preserving and protecting it.

That is a central economic truth that has not yet reached the environmentalists, perhaps because it is the opposite from the 'public' property approach with which they typically set out. It is no less true of the whole range of public services and public property from telephone booths to swimming pools, trains to schools, buses to ante-natal clinics, fire-engines to police cars, allotments to libraries, docks and quays to deck chairs and beaches, public libraries to public lavatories.

There is a sense in which government expenditure in public services conduces to a sense of social cohesion. That is when there is a feeling that we have jointly paid in taxes for a service we share in common. These are the true public goods in which we benefit one another only because we share in a service we could not enjoy at all unless we did. But when we are forced to come together to pay for services that we regard as personal, and in which misuse by others can harm us, there is no social cohesion but social tension, mutual distrust, resentment and discord. A borrower who despoils a library book, a child who defaces a classroom, an adolescent who ravages a telephone booth or railway compartment, a council tenant who neglects his house or garden, a nurse or patient who is careless with hospital equipment or crockery: these and many more do less for social cohesion than people who pay for what they want, benefit from their care of it, and suffer from their carelessness.

In the language of externalities, on which the advocates of public government services lean heavily (or too heavily), it is the user of public property who sheds external costs and damage on his unsuspecting fellow-citizens; and it is the man who pays for what he receives who bears them himself. For he internalises his externalities. And, in taking care of his own, he contributes to responsibility in the community.

* * *

Finally on this whole subject of poverty, inequality, deprivation, under-privilege and social divisiveness, I would address two questions to the many good people who still think the best solution is tax-financed free welfare and other public services.

I have argued that differences and deficiences in income should be and can be corrected by a reverse income tax to enable all in time to pay.

First, do they deny that the tax-paid system throws up other kinds of differences and deficiences that influence or decide access and distribution: in accent, social background, political influence, economic muscle?

Second, do they deny that these differences and deficiencies are more difficult to correct than are differences and deficiencies in income?

11 Administratively impracticable

Charging for goods and services, many of which have been 'free' for as long as we can remember, will seem strange, a nuisance, fussy, a new problem to think about. Prices would have to be fixed, methods of payment decided, recording and accounting organised. The fee for borrowing a book, for a term at school, for the services of a midwife, for advice on family planning, for a visit to or from a family doctor, or a week in hospital, the charge for emptying a dustbin, an hour on a tennis court, at a swimming pool, nine or eighteen holes on a golf course – all these and many more would have to be calculated. Isn't charging going to be administratively expensive, difficult, even impracticable? Shouldn't we take the word of officials who tell us that it will?

Obstruction from officials

Reluctance, resistance and obstruction may be expected from civil servants and local officials who run the existing system, and for three reasons, two bad and one (possibly) good. The first is that the present system is much easier for them. If users, customers, tenants, patients, parents pay someone in an office a long way off – the tax collector for income tax, the local authority finance officer for rates, someone even more remote and almost unidentifiable for VAT – there is no sense of obligation in taking their money, no exposure to their authority in laying down what they would like on every occasion they use a service, no physical handling of money or giving a receipt, no occasion even to say 'Thank you'. The public servant is clear of all these irksome encumbrances and can concentrate on the service he or she is 'giving'.

The second reason why we must expect resistance from public officials is that charging for private benefits will certainly disturb, probably disrupt and possibly cause upheaval in their working lives, if not sleepless nights. It could reduce their ranks by redundancy. For a change from taxing to charging would also change the very nature of their work, and require from them qualities they may not possess and will have to acquire, or change their jobs. Their relationship to the customers will have to change from that of *giver* to that of *seller*. And for that relationship they have not been trained. It is to require them to turn 180 degrees from facing colleagues who share their attitudes, hopes and lives to face their real paymasters who have a lot of other things on which to spend their money.

These two understandable reasons for obstructing charging throw doubt on the reliability of the third reason, which could conceivably be good but in practice is probably bad, or at least suspect. This objection is that charging would be unworkable, or would be so costly as to overwhelm its advantages, or cause such disturbance for such a long time as to damage the services themselves. The officials who administer the services now are, after all, the experts on the spot. No one knows more about running them than they do. Little wonder that Ministers in Whitehall and Councillors in town halls are guided as well as advised by their advisers -- their permanent officials in town-planning, housing, medicine, education, amenities and facilities, protective and environmental services. And if they said that charging in its various forms was unworkable, too costly, or disruptive we should listen to them with respect.

But there are several difficulties in the way of accepting and voting on their advice. The first I have indicated: their loyalties are in conflict. They are personally interested parties as well as expert witnesses. Their main duty may seem to be with the public they are paid to serve. But it is not easy to give advice that may shatter your daily routine and perhaps lose your job. So whatever advice they give must be checked from other sources: second opinions are as important in national policies as in personal health.

Secondly, the officials are authoritative, though not disinterested, in the running of the *existing* system of financing, but not on projected *new* systems. Their opinion on charging would be based not on experience but on conjecture -- guesswork. Being human, good husbands (or wives) and parents, and not wishing to invite or encourage an unknown technique that, after all, might work even worse than they sincerely believe, they would unconsciously tend to under-rate its probable advantages and over-state its probable disadvantages. Above all, they could not claim the same authority in advising on a new method of financing that they can properly claim in advising on the system they know from experience.

Much the same is true of the specialists in government services --

from teachers and doctors to refuse and sewage collectors (or the other way round: no order of importance is intended) – as is true of general officials and administrators. Insofar as they are in more direct personal contact with users, the effect on them might be even more cataclysmic. Their views must also, therefore, be regarded with scepticism and, where possible, double checked. Moreover they may reflect, even more than those of civil servants, local officials or general administrators, the value-judgement – which is an article of faith that does not call for logical proof – that public services are innately superior to private services because they enable the community to act together in caring for one another and especially for people in disadvantageous circumstances, in contrast to private services which create scope for individual self-seeking or profit-making at the expense of other members of society. We considered that belief in the last chapter, and the least that can be said is that it is not self-evidently true. Any official who believes that it is disbars himself to that extent from giving an authoritative and unbiased opinion.

Powers of officials in public monopolies

There is an even more disturbing tendency in the attitudes of general public officials or specialist operators that calls for early judgement by the public. If public officials and operators who regard themselves as more informed than their customers feel very strongly in favour of public services in principle, they may decide they must do what they can to dissuade or prevent the general public from adopting policies or methods they feel are not 'in the public interest', whatever the public itself may think. As a motive, at least, this is praiseworthy.

At the other extreme, officials and operators have a strong incentive to do what they can to discourage policies that endanger their livelihoods. What they can do can be very effective. Since public services are usually protected from the competition of private services, the resulting degree of monopoly enables them to enforce their opinions by stopping the services altogether. In recent times they have refused, or have announced they would refuse, to carry out the policies of government: in Manchester (Tameside) to preserve grammar schools, in Kent County to study the feasibility of a voucher experiment, in National Health Service hospitals to tend patients in pay-beds. In all episodes they were of the view that their judgement should take precedence over the intentions of a newly-elected District

Council (Tameside) and a County Council (Kent) acting within its powers (as well as over such tests of public opinion as the Ashford 'referendum' and a large public meeting) as well as national policy under law.

It may be that if officials and operators carry their opposition to government policy from adverse but reasoned advice to high-handed obstruction, their authority as advisers will be further weakened. How far their opinion, or their personal interest in maintaining their livelihood, can take precedence over the opinion or interest of people who use public services without slowing down the economy until it seizes up and preventing the working of democratic institutions – how far, in other words, employees in state-protected monopolies can go in thwarting the sovereignty of the consumer in the economy and the elector in the polity – has hardly been discussed in much depth in Britain. But it must be clear that economic systems controlled by producers must deteriorate and decline, since they resist change.

Evidence on practicability from experiment

The only reliable source of evidence is experimentation. This is the method by which mankind has tried out new ideas or techniques down the ages. Trial and error, sampling, experience, pragmatism: there are various names, some more appropriate than others, for the principle. The British are supposed to be especially wise in applying it. It seems to embody the acme of common sense. Reason points to what sounds like a good idea, but there can be no certainty about how it will work in practice. So the sane course is to try it out, on a small scale, for a time; and then, if it seems to work, extend it gradually.

There are two difficulties in this approach. One is that if the idea is tried in an untypical area or for too short a time, it may fail, because people will not react as they would to a reform expected to be nationwide and long-term; and the main idea itself may be condemned and perhaps abandoned. Professor Milton Friedman has met this difficulty with the argument that the improvement would be so marked that even an imperfect experiment could dramatise the superiority of the new method.[26] Second, opponents of the idea in principle may try to discredit it by getting in on the experiment. The risk that the idea may be destroyed because its opponents will change their tactics to 'If you can't beat 'em, join 'em' is an argument for eschewing an experiment and going for the whole hog. At its extreme this course is to introduce the idea overnight.

Step-by-step or overnight?

The step-by-step approach has been adopted in the USA. A reverse income tax has been operated for three years in New Jersey (Trenton), an education voucher for five years in California (Alum Rock). Both devices facilitated charging: the reverse tax for purchases generally, the voucher for education. Research organisations and university departments have been working on an experiment in cash housing allowances, which would facilitate charging market rents. In Australia there is to be experimentation with a housing voucher and possibly an education voucher.

The brilliant example of overnight reform is that of Professor Ludwig Erhard who introduced the new German Mark on Sunday/Monday, 20/21 June 1949, and ushered in the German 'economic miracle' that transformed desolation into affluence by liberalising and rewarding the individual will to work for self-improvement. On the other hand, the British overnight and nationwide reform, the National Health Service, has been in my view a disaster. This may sound strong language. The NHS replaced an emerging structure of charging by compulsory social insurance and taxing. It is a disaster not only because it was based on fallacious thinking: Bevan said it was 'to generalise the best', which is deceptively easy but dishonest Utopianism; if taken seriously it could be accomplished only by fearful sacrifices in housing, education, pensions, etc. (Even wiping out all defence expenditure would not suffice; it would require more than the whole national income.) The NHS is a disaster in the severely economic sense that its price in alternatives we have sacrificed is inordinate because we are stuck with it whether it performs well or badly, because its supporters judge it not by its performance – the work of fallible beings with limited materials – but by its noble goal – 'the best of everything for everyone free' – which it can never reach *and therefore never be judged as having failed*. And, in maintaining that it has not failed, its supporters keep going a system we can evidently never change by reasoned debate. ('The envy of the world', Mrs Castle has repeated, but no country in the world has copied it.) So it will go on until it collapses. And in the meantime no one counts the cost – the opportunity foregone of channelling more money into medicine by charging. No one can be sure, but the trend in spending habits as incomes rise in Britain and the experience of comparable countries in Europe, America and Australasia indicate that the real cost of the NHS is the opportunity the British have lost for decades to put more resources into medical care by developing and refining the methods of charging by co-insurance, deductibles, etc., that were emerging spontaneously before they were suppressed by Aneurin Bevan, and, even more, by his followers who could see the consequences but refused to draw the lessons.

Whatever the drawbacks, the only way of demonstrating the advantages of charging would seem to be by experimentation. The irony is that even modest experiments are opposed and obstructed by supporters of holistic, nationwide policies like the National Health Service and comprehensive education that are not easy to reverse even when they do not reach their declared aims after decades of trial. Men of all schools, with the reverence for scholarship that has sustained the Western world through adversity, must insist that reasoned argument will not be dismissed as distracting attention from perfecting schemes that require the exclusion of every new idea. Room must be found for experimentation, however administratively distracting and intellectually disturbing.

Decentralised experimentation

How can experiments in charging for hitherto 'free' public services be arranged? In Britain this task is more difficult than in other Western industrialised countries that are politically organised on a more decentralised, federal framework. In the USA, with its states, Canada, with its provinces, Germany, with its Länder, and Australia, also with its states, power is devolved to semi-sovereign regions that can initiate policies buttressed by power to raise local revenue. Regional initiative is more difficult in Britain where the counties raise local revenue to finance only a third of their expenditure, so that they have become increasingly the agents and executors of central government. Whatever they have said, or may say, in favour of decentralisation, both the Labour Party and the Conservative Party have accelerated the trend towards centralisation. In Chapter 12 I discuss the 'winds of change' in all parties that may induce or compel them (or one of their wings) to look more kindly on charging as the ultimate form of decentralisation by enfranchising individuals in the marketplace and to see it as much more effective than the political decentralisation through electoral 'representation' that is useless for personal services. In the meantime there is at least one British county that is using what powers it has to investigate new techniques in social policy.

If it persists with its readiness to abandon outdated ideas and apply new ones, Kent looks like emerging as the pioneering experimental county of the 1970s, as Birmingham was at the turn of the century, under Conservatives who call themselves Tories but who act like Whigs (as I define them). The influence of ideas on policy-making is not easy to trace: it may be long delayed, a prompter to action on long-held but subconscious intentions, or a spark that begins a new train of thought. Whatever the relationship of cause and effect in the Kent approach to experiment, it seems that a passage in *Choice in Welfare, 1970* [31] was followed by action. The passage said:

> scepticism about hypothetical social research can easily be met by experiments with a school voucher in, say, Lancashire for three years, or a health voucher in, say, Shropshire for four years, or a reverse income tax in, say, Kent (or on a smaller scale in Leeds) for three years, or a phasing out of national insurance in, say, Norfolk or Somerset for five years.

The action has been a series of experiments in Kent under John Grugeon, the 'Prime Minister' (leader of the Council), Alistair Lawton and John Barnes, 'Education Ministers' (Chairman and Vice-Chairman of the Education Committee), and Edward Moore, 'Minister for Social Services' (Chairman of the Social Services Committee). (If Opposition MPs can describe themselves by unconstitutional labels like Shadow Environment Minister, my descriptions for local politicians running a British county with a budget larger than those of nearly half the UN countries are no more pretentious than for national politicians who run nothing. The Chief Executives of the States of Australia are called 'Premier', a short form of Prime Minister, which is what they are, and their heads of departments are called Ministers. In the British tradition and unwritten constitution the form of titles is not unimportant in maintaining authority and power. In Australia the Commonwealth Prime Minister handles the state Premiers with more respect than Whitehall does County Council chairmen or party leaders.)

The Kent experiment that could most incorporate and apply the pricing (charging) principle is the education voucher, for which the Council voted nearly £10,000 for a feasibility study under academic guidance. If the voucher is regarded as earmarked puchasing power which can be used like cash to pay school fees at state or private schools, a new element of pricing will have been introduced into British education for the first time in history and the Grugeon 'Cabinet' will have showered lasting beneficial externalities over Kent and perhaps over the whole of England. The voucher can also be regarded as a certificate entitling the holder to a term's education (rather like a pensioner's free pass on a bus). As indicated briefly in Chapter 4, the voucher is a flexible instrument with the common purpose of giving the customer more authority by the new power of exit than he has in the free state system. If Kent falters, it cannot be long before the voucher is tried by another county or town urged by parents to strengthen their voice in education by the ultimate sanction of exit from unacceptable schools.

Privatisation

A second original use of pricing in Kent (as the economist sees it, though that is not how it may be regarded) is the Family Placement Project in which disturbed and sometimes delinquent adolescents of fourteen to seventeen years are placed in professional foster homes that can offer the environment of family life. Foster parents are paid around £40 a week, a contrast with the up to £100 a week of state institutions, of which the Kent County's Director of Social Services, Nicholas Stacey, said that they 'too often only increase [the adolescents'] problems and set them on the wasteful (in human and monetary terms) road to Borstal, prison or psychiatric hospital'. This scheme, thought 'greatly encouraging' so far, could denationalise the care of young people from 'public' institutions to private homes. The experiment began in March 1975 with financial help from the Gatsby Foundation for five years and with the advice and assistance of Nancy Hazel of the University of Kent at Canterbury. Four 'public' (local government) children's homes were being closed and children put into real family homes as a result of this use of pricing.

A similar experiment in 'denationalisation' (or 'privatisation' in the jargon) is a three-year scheme for moving a hundred or more lonely or enfeebled old people from public institutions into the homes of professional 'good neighbours' who are paid less than the £50–£60 it costs to keep them in an institution. Comparison with a similar area in which old (or mentally-handicapped) people are in institutions will indicate whether private family homes are better for the patient/'client' and more economic than institutional life. The scheme was estimated to cost around £200,000 including the pay of research staff, although it may in the end save even more. Financial help again came from a charity and assistance from the University of Kent. Two 'public' old-age homes were closed and old people put into real family homes.

Such schemes – at once more humane and economic – could help the county bridge the gap between Whitehall requirements, reinforced by the rising standards expected in public services, and sluggish revenue from local rates and Whitehall taxes, further widened by the increasing longevity of old and mentally handicapped people, the rising number of children placed 'in care' (sociologese for 'under the control of public officials'), the increasing number of family breakdowns reported for attention, earlier discharge from hospitals, and the increased number of battered wives, alcoholics and drug addicts publicised by pressure groups. Fostering, home helps and encouragement to voluntary bodies were the ways chosen by Kent to keep people in private family life, which in any event they preferred and which was much cheaper than public institutions. The 1976 government White Paper had indicated no growth in social expenditure for some years. The County was spending nearly £20 million on $1\frac{1}{2}$ million people, but nearly £10 million went on institutions for the few thousand.

The philosophic reflections on these measures by Edward Moore in his 1975 annual report are significant as commentaries on the less-than-scrupulous way in which citizens' tax-money has been managed by the public authorities that ostensibly husband it on their behalf.

We must ask ourselves whether we have relied upon residential care too much in the past as an 'easy way out' to solve problems. It is expensive – it means a long-term commitment to a form of service which could become out-dated because of the many restrictions which bricks and mortar and built-in facilities bring with them. This can be seen all the time when we look at out-dated hospitals and housing which, because of design deficiencies, etc., are unsuitable for the needs of the elderly and the handicapped; old persons' homes which 10-20 or more years ago represented a satisfactory way of meeting the needs of the elderly for whom we then had to care; large children's community homes which can no longer meet changing philosophies of child care. Times of economic difficulty have the effect of making those of us responsible for growth services think much more clearly about our priorities.

For John Grugeon these innovations would encourage self-reliance and voluntary effort: 'self-help, not help yourself'. Like Nicholas Stacey, he spoke of difficult adjustments in thinking and staffing. Where Stacey was talking to the staff, Grugeon was talking to the electorate: there would have to be 'very unpalatable decisions'. And he made what must be for a politician a courageous judgement: '. . . we must not treat . . . police and fire . . . in isolation. Law and order are prime points in our philosophy but not at the expense of our meagre resources'. Here was a rare recognition by a politician of the overriding limitations of scarcity and the impossibility of doing everything desirable.

The City of Lincoln, run by a Social Democratic Council, and the City of Liverpool, under a Liberal Council, have courageously raised some charges. Councillor Peppiatt and some Conservative colleagues on Thanet Council have raised charges despite obstruction and resistance. No least, there is the lone voice of Whig Councillor Margolis on Harrogate Borough Council and North Yorkshire County Council. His steady advocacy of charges for a wide range of services – Harrogate Royal Baths, the collection of derelict vehicles (previously the Council had paid the collectors), decorative lighting in shopping streets, tourist guides, colour TV aerials for council tenants, courses for pot-holers (as Bernard Levin might say, stand there while I say it again: *free courses for pot-holers*), car parking and entertainment facilities – has been resisted by Councillors, officials and local journalists with familiar unconvincing argument, but it has educated fellow Councillors, even where it has not yet inspired them to action, and earned increasing respect in the press. There may be more examples. But the scope is vast.

Everything is 'impracticable' before it is done

In his writings in the 1950s Lord Robbins said that the Inland Revenue could be relied upon to produce conclusive administrative objections to every proposal for fiscal reform (he was discussing inheritance taxes to replace death duties).[93] When Keynes proposed PAYE in 1939 the head of the Inland Revenue rejected it as administratively impracticable; two years later it was introduced. When in the 1960s there were again murmurings about the administrative nightmares of various forms of reverse income taxes to make benefits more selective and therefore higher for people in most need, Lord Houghton retorted: 'I am not put off by rude noises from government departments. I have seen too many impossibilities overcome to be discouraged by them'.[42] (He should know: he was Secretary of the Inland Revenue Staff Federation from 1922 to 1960.)

If the opponents of charging insist that it is administratively impractical, let them subject their unsupported claim to the test of experience. I have argued the case for testing their claim that the education voucher is impracticable by erecting experiments to see whether they are right. Much the same is true of charging for other public services that are not public goods – even if some of them are supposed to be. (There is even a case for experimenting with methods of linking payment by taxation to the *total* financing of public goods in which the personal benefits are not separable.) The case for experimenting in the education voucher, therefore, applies in principle to experimenting with other methods of financing – and organising – a wide range of services from health and transport on a national scale to libraries and refuse collection on a local scale. If the objectors to charging object to experiments to see whether their objections are sustained, their objections may be seen as based more on mis-guided obstruction to reform or self-interested preservation of jobs than on arguments supported by evidence.

12 Politically impossible

'Politically impossible' is the instinctive retort of the sceptic – or perhaps cynic – who senses danger to his beliefs in a new approach but does not know enough to condemn it. He therefore damns it with faint praise: 'It sounds a good idea but, of course, the people would not elect a government to act on it.' A more recent version is that, if elected, the government would be prevented by opposition from organised interests, not least, the trade unions or at least their officials, whatever their rank and file think (or even know) about it.

The danger of this reaction is that it is plausible. There are always cranks with easy solutions: visionaries, utopians, millenarians who offer prescriptions based on the two untruths that have misled mankind down the ages: that men are saints and that manna can be laid on by Ministries. I am not arguing that every crank has an inalienable right to have his brain child, or brainstorm, tried, even for a short time, at the expense of the people. The argument is deeper-lying.

The imperative conditions: imperfect man, scarce resources

Some new ideas can be sieved out as obviously contrary to sense and experience. All notions, from communism to the National Health Service, that assume man to be selfless and resources to be superabundant, must be rejected. To be taken seriously a new idea must satisfy two criteria: that it is designed for man and woman as they are, with limited vision and interests, and that it can operate with scarce resources. This means that not everything desirable – like the best of health clinics, education, housing, car parking or sports facilities – can be attained for everyone.

Yet some realistic new ideas are resisted on the spurious ground that, although desirable, they are 'politically impossible'. Charging is paying the price, paying your way, paying your penny and taking your choice; the archetypal idea that satisfies the two criteria: it recognises both human and material limitations but is designed to make the best of them. It is open, above board, does not encourage illusions, down to earth. When such a realistic and therefore practicable working idea is obstructed as 'politically impossible' we must look to the scope in civilised society for new ideas of any sort, to the structure of power that enables them to be killed before they are born, and the motives, incentives or inducements of the obstructors.

The press was silent

At first blush, the objection contradicts itself. If a new idea is in the interest of the people, it can hardly be an objection that they would reject it. If they do, the reason must be that they do not know about it. In Britain, the 'fifth estate', the press, can usually be relied on to give a sensible new idea a fair run, or even a fair wind. But here there is an odd episode in the recent press treatment of charging. There was, with a few honourable exceptions, little discussion of charging in the national press reports and comments while the world was 'waiting for Layfield' from June 1974 when the Committee to investigate local government finance[122] was appointed to May 1976 when it reported. Even the Local Government Correspondents, who are presumably knowledgeable specialists in the subject, barely referred to charging.

The Layfield lacuna

The hope that the Layfield Report would accelerate the pace of public education in the relevance of charging was dashed. It recognised the case for charging, although it made too much of the external benefits of government services, and recommended 'a review of policy and practice in charging for local services by the government and local authorities'. This review may be postponed for years or decades. But the Committee confined its recommendation that local authorities consider raising charges to the existing services because it said it had not been asked to report on which services should or should not be provided by local government.

The Committee may have been technically or legally right in concluding it could not make a recommendation on charging that might affect the structure of local services. But economically the two cannot be segregated. The Redcliffe-Maud Royal Commission reported in 1969 on the structure of local government and its services without considering its finances, which is like talking about supply and demand without considering the effect of price. The Layfield Committee in 1976 reported on financing local services without considering the effect on their scale, which is like talking about price without considering its effect on supply and demand. One more opportunity of encouraging public discussion has therefore been lost, and it will probably be at least five years before another committee of inquiry.

Fortunately, the Institute of Economic Affairs, which specialises in the micro-economic analysis of policy, has sponsored a series of studies going back to the early 1960s (listed in the References) that provide the best (or only) collection of succinct analyses as a scholarly background to a public discussion that I hope *Charge* will further stimulate. Appendix I briefly explains the method and results, discussed below.

The question remains: If a new idea is in the interest of the people, why should the people reject it? My reply is that what politicians (or academics or anyone else who claims to know public opinion) mean when they say charging is politically impossible is either that they themselves do not like charging or that they are incapable of showing the public to see it is for their benefit. At bottom the 'politically impossible' objection conceals a failure of political education and a failure to resist pressure groups.

I base these conclusions on the emerging insights from the new theory of public choice which analyses politics in terms of 'the vote motive'[114] and on the results of the four IEA surveys of public reaction to priced alternatives in state and private education, medicine, housing and pensions.[31, 77] The theory of public choice is complemented by the theory of bureaucracy, also developed mostly by American economists. (Appendix 2 indicates the main sources.)

Public preferences unknown to politicians

The four IEA surveys have a significant origin. They were prompted by the very objection of 'politically impossible' made by people of various political colours against the early IEA Papers on pensions, housing and medical care. It was said that, although their authors made cogent cases, there was no hope that their reasoning or conclusions would have any effect on policy because, the politicians thought, they were not politically *profitable*. Since IEA authors have always been asked to pursue their analysis wherever it led them without regard for what was politically expedient, this reaction was interpreted as a compliment, but with the danger that it would discourage academics from pursuing studies that might have important long-term results whatever their immediate prospects.

Moreover, it begged the question of what was possible politically. Scholars must, of course, be concerned with analysing what is right, not with what will produce immediate popularity for this or that party. But politicians are not a neutral part of the political process. They cannot reflect public wishes unless they also educate the public in the policies between which it can choose. Their competence is in question if they cannot apply good ideas that are in the public interest.

In the post-war economic climate of Keynesian macro-economic thinking (which Keynes, who died in 1946, might have rejected) politicians gave little time to micro-economic thinking, which they tend to pooh-pooh as rather old-fashioned. They did not recognise its explosive, revolutionary power as a critique of government in general and the size and structure of British government. They did not see its exciting potential for liberating policy, and in particular enfranchising the poor and the under-privileged in the second half of the twentieth century, who have been submerged and repressed in the developing structure of free services

To test the politicians' hypothesis (or rationalisation of inaction) the IEA asked Mass Observation in 1962 to see how far it could discover opinion and potential reaction to alternative policies of higher taxes for better state benefits and lower taxes with charges for alternative private education, medical care and pensions. In the previous fifteen years or so since the creation of the post-war stage of the Welfare State, polls and surveys had claimed to discover overwhelming general support for 'free' tax-paid state welfare. The first Mass Observation survey in 1963 found otherwise; so did further surveys in 1965 and 1970. [Appendix 1] The reason was that it introduced realistic prices by using the micro-economic device of the voucher (for education and medicine) in discovering people's preferences and emphasised costs and taxes in a parallel series of macro-economic questions on government policy in general.

Essentially the micro-economic questions asked whether heads of families would take a voucher valued at one-third or two-thirds of state school fees and add to it to pay for education of their choice. A similar question covered vouchers to pay for health insurance. The three successive surveys found a gradually increasing proportion in every social class interested in or anxious for choice, even at the expense of dipping into their pockets. The macro-economic questions showed the same trend. A survey of reactions to housing policy led by the late Professor F.G. Pennance, on broadly comparable lines, found similar reactions.[77]

This was evidence – hypothetical and circumstantial, but nevertheless more scientific than any others – that reform in existing policies was, after all, *not* politically impossible. It came as no surprise to Ralph Harris and me. As economists with a strongly micro approach, we had always thought that the 'price-less' surveys (still being used) were of no significance. What surprised us was the large proportion – a third, rising to two-fifths and a half – indicating a desire for something different from what the politicians had been giving them.

Disbelief

The instinctive reaction of some who did not welcome the findings was to question the technical accuracy of the surveys. The late Richard Crossman (badly advised) went further and suggested in the *Guardian* that pensioners and women had been omitted from the sample because they might not give the required replies. (He later publicly withdrew the insinuation.) Academics, mostly sociological, journalists and others to whom the findings were unexpected and unwelcome, found technical fault but did not disturb our general discovery that, *if investigated through charging*, the public was not as frozen in its attitudes as were politicians out of touch with its underlying preferences. The protesters may be judged to have resorted to the 'politically impossible' objection in order to resist reform they disliked on philosophic grounds (Labour), or emotional grounds (Liberals), or traditional grounds (Conservatives). Not for the first time, political leaders were shown up as being a long way behind their followers. They were simply out of touch – because they did not understand the price system. What they asserted as 'politically impossible' was not only politically desirable but – if they were not blinkered – could evidently be politically popular and politically profitable.

It was also now clear that the conventional method of discovering public opinion through the ballot box had concealed rather than revealed it. To record mass votes in favour of free welfare from voters not told their costs proved nothing. Charging was the only way to discover preferences, as well as the way in which to finance the services the public wanted.

If the politicians are obstructing a reform that reason indicates is for the benefit of the public, and a reform, moreoever, that the public shows it would welcome, the objection of politically impossible becomes a strange phenomenon. Economists have to examine the role of the politician more closely in the effort to see why he is reluctant to perform the task, for which he is elected and paid, of providing the people with the institutions they prefer. The new theory of public choice is shedding more light as it develops. The central insight that has emerged so far is that the politician is most fruitfully analysed in terms of his electoral interests. And if those interests do not necessarily conflict with the benefit of the public, neither do they necessarily coincide with them.

The entry of economists into the realm of what will seem to be politics is an aspect of their 'imperialist' tendency in recent years to be concerned not only with buying and selling, but also with subjects not conventionally regarded as within their province: charity, government, tax avoidance and evasion, marriage, crime, and others. In a sense, after being used or misused by politicians, economists are turning the tables on them by examining them more closely and critically. In the process much of the mystique of statesmanship and the self-importance of the politician may be blown away. I fancy he has been rumbled and, unless he enslaves us all first, will play a more humble role in the future. (Professor W.H. Hutt, another of the economists who have rebelled against early teaching that the solution to social problems lay in the state, has penetrating insights in a little book called *Politically Impossible...?*[45])

Politically impassable?

But the road to that fair city will require skilful negotiating, not least because the politicians, and their acolytes and attendants, the officials, bureaucrats, employees, advisers and retainers, will put up a barrage of road blocks painted 'Politically Imp*a*ssable.' I have long been intrigued by the processes that decide whether new ideas are translated into policy or are ignored, neglected and forgotten. If it is permissible to think of ideas as contending with one another, they seem to require a range of techniques to achieve acceptance: they must influence thinkers and scholars fundamentally in the long run, politicians and public servants with power in the short run, and the communications media and the literati in the medium run. Ideas thus require intellectual long-range 'artillery' and lobbying short-range 'infantry.' The academic case for charging in general, and for the voucher as a device for introducing it as one instrument in particular, has been made for fifteen years or more by the intellectual 'artillery'. But there was little interest from politicians until recently, when a company of 'infantry' went into action in one sector of the field. Their activities are relevant in judging the objection of 'political impossibility'.

The 'infantry' company of women

The possibility of translating ideas into policy is indicated by what may prove to be a significant chapter in education policy that has lessons for public policy in general. In April 1974 a resolution proposing experiments in the voucher was prepared for the conference of the National Council of Women (NCW) and in October received a majority vote in support but not enough for the two-thirds required to make it NCW policy. The motion was moved by Marjorie Seldon, daughter and niece of pertinacious social reformers, who had advocated vouchers in various writings,[108] and seconded by Margaret Jones, a teacher. It was opposed mainly by union representatives of teachers.

(I must declare a family connection. Marjorie Seldon is my wife. The difference between the success of independent schools in nurturing academic skills in pupils in the middle and lower range of intellect, and the unnecessarily low expectations of teacher, pupil and parent in the non-selective state schools, had developed her interest in the voucher. She wrote in the Liberal magazine *New Outlook* in 1966: 'The problem is to extend choice to *all*: to the children of the bus driver, shop assistant and widow as well as of the stockbroker, University teacher, or politician . . . There is a danger that ability to pay is being replaced by ability to persuade. The best bargains in schooling may go to those with the 'know how', the command of English, or of the political strings . . . The voucher would give buying power that speaks the same language irrespective of social class.')

In October 1974 the Kent County Council majority party (Conservative) said in an election manifesto that it was interested in the possibility of an experiment in the education voucher. In January 1975 a handful of NCW enthusiasts formed the Friends of the Education Voucher Experiment in Representative Regions (FEVER) with Marjorie Seldon as Chairman, Ruth Garwood Scott, a former headmistress, as her main aide, and a Committee of five women: a social worker, a teacher, a nurse, a lawyer, and a social survey interviewer. Several months were spent on the familiar methods of gathering public support traditional in British social reform. FEVER made impressive progress, ultimately recognised by the BBC in a TV programme, educating the public and discovering wide support for experiments among parents of all classes, not least in working-class areas with little choice of school, and among educationists, religious leaders, teachers and MP's.

Academic examination of the voucher was continued in two further IEA Papers based on material prepared for the Layfield Committee, which had asked the IEA for evidence on charging and on the voucher as a means of raising revenue: one paper was based on the written evidence on types of voucher, economic effects, administrative aspects, etc by Alan Maynard[66] : the other was based on oral evidence on charging for local government services in general and on vouchers in particular by Ralph Harris and me.[32] In February 1976 Kent County Council announced that it would conduct a feasibility study for an experiment.

The significant lessons of this pioneering in opening up, and persuading people in political power to consider, a radical new idea are mainly five:

(i) Academic analysis is a necessary prelude to consideration by authority, but it requires 'activist' publicity and propaganda to stimulate public discussion in the press, which politicians too often regard as reflecting or making public opinion.

(ii) The voucher has been opposed, without any evidence at all, by the officials of teachers' unions on the general ground that it would damage education; yet all they could feel, or fear, was that it might disturb the system with which they identified their own, or their members', interests.

(iii) Such people have opposed the voucher not only in principle but also as an experiment that would reveal whether their objections were well founded. This is a particularly reprehensible attitude from teachers trained to respect scholarship and the open mind.

(iv) The weight attached, even by Kent County Council Conservatives, to teachers' opinions indicates the weakness of the consumer in a price-less, 'free' system vis-à-vis the supplier. Without charges to indicate costs, identify the paymaster, and empower him to enforce his preferences, the piper does not call the tune: the consumer is thwarted by the employee he pays.

(v) The voucher was condemned, dismissed or ignored by journalists (Education Correspondents) caught up in reporting the existing system whatever its defects. Some evidently could not contemplate education financed in any other way than taxation. It is clear that a lot of effort must be put into educating those whom the public regards as the experts.

Pressure groups suppress individuals

The politician believes that some new ideas are politically impossible because he interprets public opinion at second remove through the newspapers and TV and the vocal activists in occupational organisations, political parties and pressure groups.

As long as services are organised and financed by government, it is administratively simplest to negotiate with the officials of organisations - unions of postmen and porters, teachers and doctors – since it cannot consult all their members, still less non-members. The convenience is clear. The danger – that the officials will act as a barrier between government and members rather than a link – is less clear. It is even clearer that government will pay more attention to the organised voice of the producer – in transport, fuel, schools, hospitals, refuse-collection, postal services, libraries – than of the consumer, who is usually not organised at all. The Patients' Association, Parent-Teacher Associations and other groups do what they can on general rules and procedures, but they cannot speak for individual patients or parents, most of whom, especially the self-effacing, do not join such bodies. Those who do are the more articulate who need them least. The Conservative solution of parent-governors reflects the middle-class failure to see that the voice of the working-class parent cannot be 'represented'; it cannot be equalised with that of the articulate, well-connected, socially adroit, middle-class parent; it can be made effective only by the sanction of withdrawing purchasing power. The voice, even if equal, can be made effective only if it is supplemented by an exit. No-one listens very hard to the man (or woman) who cannot escape.

There seems no way out of the 'politically impossible' *impasse* except by organisations such as FEVER that set out not to 'represent' individuals but to obtain reforms that will provide machinery – in this case the voucher – by which individuals of all kinds, most of all the least influential or articulate, *can represent themselves*.

The objection of 'politically impossible' thus resolves itself into a damaging critique of the very institutions the objectors are trying to preserve by obstructing reform: the self-protective reaction of the vast structure of private interests locked in the public services. And financing these services by charging is the only way of rearranging them to suit the people for whom they are intended – ultimately by giving them the power of *exit* to make their voice heard, initially by empowering them with a more effective *voice* to require that the service for which they pay by taxes shall match their preferences, and not be misused to create or preserve jobs for public 'servants'.

The external damage of government expenditure

It is now time to turn the tables on the 'politically impossible' obstructionists and consider whether it may not be the conventional policies of increasing government expenditure financed by rising taxation that are becoming politically impossible.

Even if it could be demonstrated that on all five secondary grounds – the pretexts of poverty, irresponsibility, externality, economy and monopoly – services should be provided by government whether they were public goods or not, the repercussions, the external damage on people and institutions, must be weighed in the decision. Here I discuss three main forms of damage; others are reviewed in other chapters.

The first is the increasing concentration of power in government that would spread from economic activity to political institutions, civil rights and freedom of expression. The general tendency is for the exclusion of independent activity in supplying public services to be followed by the restriction of independent activity in other spheres – political, literary, cultural.

So I would argue. But the advocates of increasing government authority over economic activity would deny it and nothing will convince them otherwise. There is a vast literature on both sides of the argument. For me the evidence is plain enough, in communist as well as capitalist societies from Russia to Sweden. It is true that we in Britain have reached the point at which, although 60 per cent of the GNP (as calculated until recently) is disposed of by government, yet political and civil liberties largely remain. But there are two errors in the argument. First, we have not been here long. In 1970 the figure was 50 per cent and in 1960 40 per cent. An increase of 20 per cent in sixteen years will take time to work its way through political institutions. Second, the increase has mostly been not in cash benefits returned to individual citizens and spent by them (about 20 per cent of GNP), but in direct control over the production of goods and services. If the 40 per cent of direct control over men and machines and land continues to grow, the political repercussions cannot lie far behind. The avenues for *independent* activity in fuel, transport, education, medicine, postal services and elsewhere have been closed, or are closing. These are now wholly or largely state activities. People who could offer the public better services for private profit in competition with others have been regarded as disturbing public services. It may not be long before they are denounced as enemies of the state.

The second form of damage lies in the burgeoning bureaucracy. Here the growth is less steep but also relatively recent. The total labour force grew between 1959 and 1974 from 23.84 million to 25.11 million, by 5.7 per cent. Total government employees rose from 5.84 to 6.84 million. In 1959 the proportion was 25 per cent of the total labour force, in 1974 27 per cent. It is higher in 1977 than it was in 1974, and will be higher in 1980 if more industry is run by government, directly or through nominally independent public corporations, if all independent education, medicine and other services are outlawed, and if independence in the professions and trading is further repressed and its practitioners, from architects and actuaries to small business men and shopkeepers, take refuge in public employment.

Third, the repercussions of continued expansion in public services are so far most evident in the effects of the rising taxation required to finance them. The long-hallowed liberal tradition of the British is that the law is sacred and is to be obeyed. Anyone who does not like it must not break it but persuade his fellow-Britons to change it by constitutional procedure. In the last five or ten years it has become increasingly doubtful whether this is still the generally accepted British attitude to the law on taxes. Britain is nearer to lawlessness in public as well as private life than at any time I can recall. The readiness to pay taxes legislated by Parliament has been eroded by party-political acceptance (or encouragement) of resistance to, or open defiance of, law elsewhere – the law on rent in Clay Cross, the law on peaceful picketing by flying pickets, the law on unions by shop stewards, the law on property by sit-ins, the law on maintaining postal and other public services by a trade union, and others. Law is unenforceable unless it is generally accepted as just: fines or imprisonment cannot be imposed on thirty million taxpayers.

If several hundred trade union officials or several hundred thousand public servants or nationalised employees think the law threatens their jobs, the much larger number of taxpayers (that is, all earners and spenders) seem to be feeling increasingly that the tax laws threaten their livelihoods, their families, their ways of life, and their values. They see government responding to the strike-threat of monopoly unions, not least in public employment. Rate-payers have protested. Taxpayers generally are reacting differently. Tax evasion is spreading in Britain, and it is not because the British are changing their moral standards from within; it is directly related to the continual increase in taxation required to provide unnecessary public services in recent years. And insofar as public services are not public goods, the politically-created deterioration in moral standards is another unnecessary but damaging externality of the failure to finance them by charging.

The high price of high taxes

The persistent effort to finance private benefits by taxes seems to be exacting a high price that the British have never been asked if they are prepared to pay – the weakening respect for law and the weakening confidence in representative political institutions. If, by raising taxes *unnecessarily*, politicians have forced the traditionally law-abiding British into breaking the law by tax evasion, then the law-makers can be judged no more moral than the tax-payers who break it. Politicians have not only created irresistible pressures to law-breaking; they also expect civil servants (tax-collectors) to enforce an unenforceable law and they require citizens to inform on one another.

The will of the people?

The moral authority of the law rests on the consent of the people, normally interpreted in Britain as a simple electoral majority. The morality of even a majority is dubious. Legal coercion of a minority by a majority is unavoidable, we have seen, for public goods. But, we have also seen, some two-thirds of British public services are not public goods. To this extent the minority is coerced *unnecessarily*. Even so, Professor Gordon Tullock argues, a simple (50.1 per cent) majority is not efficient in indicating general assent where bargains have to be struck by groups in democratic systems ('log-rolling').[114] He argues that 'reinforced majorities' of two-thirds should be used more widely. This rule would profoundly change British political institutions, though the reasoning underlying it is gradually finding its way into scholarly text-books. (We need hardly recall that the German people had given Hitler a majority in the 1933 Reichstag: Fascism, with all its works, was therefore 'legal' and 'democratic'.)

But British governments have had their moral authority reduced in the thirty years since the war, when the vast expansion of non-public 'public' services took place, because no government has had a majority of votes cast, still less of the electorate that could have voted. The highest percentage of votes cast was 49.74 per cent for the Conservatives in 1955; and that was 38.18 per cent of the electorate. At the last General Election, in October 1974, Labour attracted 39.29 per cent of the votes cast, or 28.62 per cent of the electorate. (Table A). A party that attracts less than two in five of the votes cast, and not much more than one in four of all voters, can hardly speak with the moral authority of a government that attracts 60 or 70 per cent of voters in an election with a choice of parties.

A truer representation

Professor Tullock argues that in a multi-party system, which we have had since 1974 when the Liberals attracted nearly 20 per cent of votes cast, the wings of each party tend to diverge. If, instead of the barely distinguishable high-government-expenditure-for-state-welfare of both parties, the elector had been able to decide between the two philosophies of paternalism (with free services) and liberal individual responsibility (with charging), the votes in 1974 and the policies since then might have been very different. If the wings had been able to declare their policies openly, instead of suppressing them in internal party coalitions, the position might have been as in Table G to reflect more faithfully the underlying attitudes of the British people to state control, nationalisation, taxation, universal or selective welfare, bureaucracy, trade union power, independent initiative. There could have been a majority of 66 per cent for liberal individual responsibility and a minimal (lower taxes with charging) state and a minority of 27 per cent for paternalist collectivism (free services with higher taxes). The wings might then have formed a new coalition, outside the old

TABLE G: BRITISH POLITICAL OPINION – A TRUER RESULT

	1974 (October) General Election vote for conventional party (% of votes cast)		Suggested vote for wing with identifiable philosophy
Conservative	36	Whig	22
		Tory	14
Labour	39	Social Democrat	34
		Socialist	5
Liberal	18	Libertarian	10
		Paternalist	8

party boundaries, perhaps temporarily until the state had been rolled back.

There is no technical difficulty in raising the state proportion of GNP from 40 per cent to 50, to 60, to 70, to 80. But I would say that beyond about 20 to 25 per cent it can be done only with increasing coercion in the face of intensifying resentment, resistance and defiance. That, broadly, is what seems to have happened since World War II, and especially since 1964. The two main parties may have believed sincerely that a 'high-government-taxation-for-state-welfare' policy is what the British wanted; but they were misled by the defective electoral system based on price-less, 57-variety, full-line forcing of all-or-nothing political platforms that prevented voters from indicating opinion on single issues (from continued subsidies for relatively high-income Council tenants to price-indexed pensions for public servants). When they found by subsequent micro-economic reaction that the people did not want to pay high taxes, they should have stopped expanding public services long ago to discover where and why they had gone wrong. The electorate may have voted for state welfare because they did not know its price; they did not vote for a police state.

Supporters of the legalistic theory, or legal fiction, that whatever the state passes into law is moral and must be enforced, however high the cost, will probably have to meet increasing resistance based, perhaps unconsciously, on a sense of 'natural justice' that there must be much more than 39 per cent (or 29 per cent) of voters in favour of high taxes to justify enforcing them on the majority of 61 per cent (or 71 per cent).

A numbered summary

Having completed the argument for charging and rejected the objections, I restate the main propositions.

1 Only about a third of British government expenditure is on public services necessarily financed by taxes because they are public goods.

2 Most public services yield separable private services that could be more efficiently financed by charges.

3 They have been brought into government production for five reasons that are largely or wholly insufficient.

   i Poverty: can be treated better on the demand side by a reverse income tax; only about half, probably less, of all taxes go to redistribute income; the rest is 'abortive'. Differences or deficiencies in income can be remedied more easily than differences in social background, political influence, or economic muscle in the access to free, tax-financed services. Moreover, the poor are not always the main users of the public services: higher education, sports amenities, etc. They would therefore be the gainers if public services that government did not have to provide were not provided by government at all.

   ii Irresponsibility: could be removed if 'irresponsible' people were taught to exercise discretion and judgement by benefits in cash or voucher instead of being given 'free' benefits in kind that do not teach choice but habituate them to passive acceptance.

   iii Economy: even where government services reduce cost by avoiding duplication, the better method is private organisation and management subject to minimal government regulation until technical innovation restores smaller-scale operation; but often state costs are higher than costs in competitive markets.

   iv Externality: the argument for government 'free' provision of education etc. is unsubstantiated and often nebulous; social benefits can often be ensured by cash grants or earmarked vouchers to consumers.

   v Monopoly: government control tends to perpetuate monopoly

by exposing government to importunity from vested interests; again the better method is often private organisation and management subject to government regulation until technical innovation restores competition.

4 Charges would yield revenue for public services that could not be raised by government through taxation. Free services are sparser and inferior to paid-for services.

5 Charges would improve the efficiency of public services by subjecting them to consumer sovereignty and eventual producer competition.

6 Charges would increase the total resources channelled to services of which more were demanded than could be financed through taxation.

7 Taxation is the only method of financing true public goods, but it is still a second best because it does not indicate personal preferences.

8 Unnecessary taxation generates its own external costs:

  i Progressive restriction of initiative independent of the state and, in time, of constitutional and civil liberties as the expansion in government expenditure works its way through political institutions.

  ii Progressive expansion of non-productive bureaucracy at the expense of productive industry.

  iii A weakening in the respect for law; deterioration of moral standards, social divisiveness between public servants and the public; corruption of bureaucracy.

9 The machinery of representative democracy has been extended from public goods, where it is unavoidable but defective, to private benefits, where it is avoidable and inefficient, and where it unnecessarily but irremediably prejudices lower-income people with little or no social connections, political influence or economic muscle.

10 New machinery has to be devised to decide the public will in public goods by referenda and in private benefits by markets.

11 The sectional and occupational resistances to charging could be overcome by public opinion.

12 The existing alignment of British political parties could be replaced by a realignment according to attitudes to 'public' services and public goods and to the resulting policies on taxation, nationalisation, bureaucracy, consumer authority, choice, competition.

Appendices

True and false measures
of public preferences

In Britain there are only two ways of measuring what the public wants: in the ballot box and the market. The ballot box records votes by crosses cast for this or that party, policy or politician. The market records votes by money paid for this or that commodity, service, brand, firm or business man.

The ballot box is crude compared with the market. The ballot box is used locally every three and nationally up to five years; the market is used every day or few days (for food, newspapers, transport, etc), every few months (clothes, books, etc) or years (furniture, homes, etc).

The ballot box says: 'This is my list of 57 varieties: take it or leave it.' The market says: 'This is my one item: pay for as much or as little as you want.' (Motto, p. 2.)

The ballot box says: 'This is what we promise.' The market says: 'What you see before your very eyes is what you take away if you pay.'

The ballot box says: 'Aren't our party slogans splendid!' The market says: 'Judge us by your experience of our product.'

The ballot box says: 'We are saints, public-spirited, selfless and honest. The others are devils, in the pay of vested interests, selfish, dishonest.' The market says: 'We are the best. Compare our value, quality, price.'

The ballot box says: 'Look! Benefits galore! All Free!' The market says: 'All our goods are priced; tax shown separately.'

This contrast is over-simplified but basically right. Even if allowance is made for advertising, the persuasion of people to try this rather than that breakfast cereal, washing powder or newspaper is infinitely harmless contrasted with the persuasion to 'buy' this or that political slogan, promise or policy. You can, with little loss, change from one cereal, powder or paper to another every few days. But you are stuck with the wrong political policy for years or a lifetime (no matter how bad it becomes, the NHS will go on and on and on).

Although the ballot box is very much a second best to the market, it must be used for public goods because opinion on, say, how much and what quality of defence, cannot easily be measured in the market by

TABLE H: PREFERENCES DISCOVERED BY EDUCATION AND HEALTH VOUCHERS, 1970

(i) Proportions accepting £75 or £150 education voucher for each child (sample of people with children of school age under 19)

	Socio-economic group			
	Highest	High-Medium	Low-Medium	Lowest
			%	
£75 voucher, requiring £150 in cash	38	29	26	21
£150 voucher, requiring £75 in cash	52	49	42	35

(ii) Proportions accepting £7 or £10 health voucher for each member of household

			%	
£7 voucher, requiring £7 in cash	29	32	25	22
£10 voucher, requiring £5 in cash	36	38	29	26

individuals voting with their money. But even where there are private benefits, the ballot box is still used because wrong thinking brought it into being and vested interests keep it going even where it is inferior to the market.

It has given wrong results because it has not used prices where it supplies private benefits that could be priced. Political elections (and private polls) have asked the electorate as a whole (or samples) to say whether they preferred this or that public service — say, state education, the NHS, council housing. But to ask 'Do you prefer A to B?' is *meaningless unless you know their prices*. You will prefer A if it costs much less than B, and B if it costs much less than A. General Elections ask for meaningless answers because political policies have no prices. They do not ask 'How much more defence would you like at £100 more in taxes per family for each aircraft carrier or air-to-ground missile?' And private polls that are price-less are similarly useless: not surprisingly they 'found' large support for ('free') state this, that and the other.

The only attempts in Britain to discover preferences in the personal benefits in the so-called 'public' services were made by the IEA in 1963, 1965 and 1970 for education, health and pensions and in 1968 for housing. Instead of the fruitless question 'Do you prefer state or private education, health, pensions, housing?' the IEA questions put a price-tag on the alternatives by using the voucher as the way to show the cost of a choice between state and private services. Thus in 1970 it asked 'If (instead of 'free' state education) the Government gave you £75 a year for each child aged 11 or more which could only be spent on education − and you would have to pay another £150 yourself to make up the fees − would you accept the offer or not?' It also asked what people would do if the offer was £150 to be topped up by £75. A comparable question was asked for health insurance premiums as for school fees: £7 for each person, to be topped up by £7; and £10 to be topped up by £5. The results were fascinating. Preferences (not surprisingly to the economist) were revealed as varying with price (the addition of money required to top them up).

This, although only approximate, is a fascinating glimpse into the preferences suppressed for many decades that lie below the layers of cotton wool of the welfare state. It showed, *for the first time since the welfare state was created*, the *true* state of public wishes that are ignored and frustrated by 'free' welfare.

This method of discovering preferences was acknowledged as the right way, in principle, to investigate public demand for welfare services by the (Social Democratic) Professor Mark Blaug and (Liberal) Professor Jack Wiseman and the Conservative (Tory) Timothy Raison. But no political party has followed it through.

A note on further readings

Readers who want to go into the subject more fully will find the following helpful on (i) public goods, (ii) charging and (iii) the economic debate generally.

(i) *The nature of public goods.* The most systematic short analysis is Professor Maurice Peston's *Public Goods and the Public Sector.*[82] A somewhat longer, in parts more difficult, but more recent and rewarding discussion is Professor C. K. Rowley's and Professor Alan T. Peacock's *Welfare Economics: A Liberal Restatement.*[100] Readers will see that the position in *Charge* is nearer the latter.

An easier book is Professor Gordon Tullock's *Private Wants, Public Means,*[113] and a more difficult one Professor Mancur Olson's *The Logic of Collective Action,*[71] sub-titled 'Public Goods and the Theory of Groups'. A British book that discusses the externalities of economic growth, and is also a complement to *Private Wants, Public Means,* is Dr E. J. Mishan's pioneering *The Costs of Economic Growth,*[69] a much more sophisticated analysis of social costs than that of the environmentalists who would lose the baby of economic growth with the bath water of externalities. (Since both Tullock and Mishan ascribe the origin of their books to me, I shall not take sides, but readers will see with which I agree more.)

Charity as a public good is discussed by Professor Thomas R. Ireland and David B. Johnson in *The Economics of Charity.*[46, 50]

The reader will be diverted by Professor Richard B. McKenzie's and Professor Gordon Tullock's *The New World of Economics,*[62] which discusses public goods in the course of applying economics to its new subjects of learning, politics, crime, the family, etc.

Most of the new thinking on the nature and implications of public goods is published in *Public Choice,* the journal of the Center for the Study of Public Choice at the Virginia Polytechnic Institute and State University, Blacksburg, Virginia, USA, whose Senior Editor is Professor Tullock.

(ii) *Charging.* As a much-neglected subject, the literature is scattered and patchy. The References list a good source for each 'public' service. The main sources are IEA Papers and US journals and books. British periodicals and publishers have been backward in seeing the potentialities of the subject.

(iii) *General.* A good first entry to general economic policy on public goods is (liberal)* Professor Lord Robbins' latest book, *Political Economy Past and Present*,[94] accurately sub-titled 'a review of leading theories of economic policy'. It discusses the classical theory of 'collective' goods with 'indiscriminate' benefits. Readers might then dip into (Whig) Professor Hayek's *magnum opus, The Constitution of Liberty.*[34]

Two books for the general reader are by parents and son: (liberal) Professor Milton and Rose Friedman's readable *Capitalism and Freedom*;[24] (Adam Smith liberal) David Friedman's *The Machinery of Freedom*, subtitled 'Guide to a Radical Capitalism',[23] discusses the nature of public goods incisively. Samuel Brittan's *Capitalism and the Permissive Society*[7] discusses public goods in a British setting. Professor J. E. Meade's *The Just Economy*[67] is the most recent discussion by a 'liberal socialist' (Social Democrat).

The nature and indispensability of pricing is analysed by the Swedish (Social Democratic) economist Professor Assar Lindbeck in a short and easy book addressed to the 'New Left' which thinks the world could dispense with prices and run on goodwill, *The Political Economy of the New Left.*[59]

The importance of charging in giving consumers an exit as well as a voice, or an exit to make voice effective, emerges from Professor Albert O. Hirschmann's *Exit, Voice and Loyalty.*[40]

Professor George J. Stigler's latest book, *The Citizen and the State*,[112] will illuminate thinking on the competence of the state in regulating what in Britain are called nationalised industries and 'public' corporations that are not allowed to charge market rates for political reasons. He writes with his customary wit and lucidity.

The principles underlying the financing and organisation of the post office, education, justice, police, fire, roads and money are racily discussed by William C. Wooldridge in *Uncle Sam, the Monopoly Man.*[119]

Two more philosophic works that question the competence or

* These philosophic labels are used by the authors about themselves.

relevance of the state in providing services are Professor Sir Karl Popper's *The Open Society and its Enemies*[89] and Professor Robert Nozick's *Anarchy, State and Utopia.*[70]

Professor Harry G. Johnson's *On Economics and Society*[51] has illuminating passages and pages on public goods and the implications for policy.

Sweden is often quoted as the ideal society that controls essential services by government in the public interest. This impression is largely destroyed by Roland Huntford's *The New Totalitarians.*[44]

Readers who want a handwork of reference to economic concepts should have a dictionary of economics. I should be less than candid if I did not say that, although there are several on the British market with varying virtues, readers of this book would find most helpful the in-depth but still short essays in *Everyman's Dictionary of Economics.*[107]

Several US journals have in recent years vigorously reappraised the argument and evidence on the control and financing of 'public' services:

The Public Interest, 10 East 53 Street, New York, 10022.
Publishes impressive rethinking of conventional attitudes and policies. (There is no British equivalent.)

Commentary, a comparable journal, 165 East 56 Street, New York, 10022.

Intercollegiate Review, 14 South Bryn Mawr Avenue, Bryn Mawr, Penn, 19010.
Published by the Intercollegiate Studies Institute; circulates mainly in American universities.

The Alternative, P.O. Box 877, Bloomington, Indiana 47401
An 'intellectual' journal published by students; maintains a high standard.

Reason, P.O. Box 6157, Santa Barbara, California 93111
A monthly, intellectually stimulating.

Libertarian Review, 6737 Annapolis Road, P.O. Box 2599, Landover Hills, Maryland 20784.
A monthly, with one or two longish review-essays but mainly shorter reviews.

The Centre for Libertarian Studies, Suite 50, 200 West 58th Street, New York, NY 10019, publishes a news letter and the *Journal of Libertarian Studies.*

Laissez-faire books, 208A Mercier Street, New York, NY 10012, regularly distributes a wide-ranging catalogue, covering history, economics and philosophy.

Postscript

After *Charge* was completed I learned of a book by Professor R. M. Bird of the University of Toronto on very much the same subject, *Charging for Public Services*, but couched in rather more economic/technical language. It was published in December 1976 by the Canadian Tax Foundation, Toronto. It seems a most sophisticated and persuasive discussion, set in the Canadian context, of the principles and their application to policy. Professor Bird's object is the same as mine: to inform public discussion because, like me, he thinks that the main obstacle to charging is not that the case is unsubstantiated but that there is not sufficient public understanding of it because vested interests will oppose it. I strongly recommend it to readers of *Charge* who want to go into the subject more fully.

April, 1977

References

Index

References

1 Beckerman, W., *Pricing for Pollution*, IEA, 1975.
2 Bentham, J., *Manual of Political Economy*, 1825.
3 Bird, P.A., and Jackson, C.I., 'Economic Charges for Water', in *The Theory and Practice of Pricing*, IEA, 1967.
4 Blake, Lord (with Patten, J.), Eds., *The Conservative Opportunity*, Macmillan, 1976.
5 Blaug, M., 'The Economics of Education in English Classical Political Economy', in *Essays on Adam Smith*, University of Glasgow, 1976.
6 Brittan, S., *Left or Right: The Bogus Dilemma*, Secker & Warburg, 1968.
7 Brittan, S., *Capitalism and the Permissive Society*, Macmillan, 1975.
8 Buchanan, J.M. (with Tullock, G.), *The Calculus of Consent*, University of Michigan Press, 1962.
9 Buchanan, J.M., *The Inconsistencies of the N.H.S.*, IEA, 1965.
10 Buchanan, J.M., *Public Finance in Democratic Process*, University of North Carolina Press, 1967.
11 Buchanan, J.M., *Demand and Supply of Public Goods*, Rand McNally & Co (USA), 1968.
12 Buchanan, J.M., *The Limits of Liberty*, University of Chicago Press, 1975.
13 Burke, E., *An Appeal from the New to the Old Whigs* (1791), Bobbs, Merrill (USA), 1962.
14 Carmichael, J., *Vacant Possession*, IEA, 1964.
15 Carter, R.L., 'Pricing and the Risk of Fire', in *The Theory and Practice of Pricing*, IEA, 1967.
16 Carter, R.L., *Theft in the Market*, IEA, 1974.
17 Coleraine, Lord, *For Conservatives Only*, Stacey, 1970.
18 Crosland, A., 'The Long-term Future of Public Expenditure,' Fabian Lecture, *Guardian*, 24 March 1976.
19 Crossman, R.H.S., *Inside View: Three Lectures on Prime Ministerial Government*, Jonathan Cape, 1972.

20 Diamond, Lord, *Public Expenditure in Practice*, Allen & Unwin, 1975.
21 Dolan, E.G., *TANSTAAFL (There Ain't No Such Thing As A Free Lunch)*, Holt, Rinehart & Winston (NY), 1971.
22 Freeman, Roland, *Municipal Review*, April 1976.
23 Friedman, D., *The Machinery of Freedom*, Harper & Row (NY), 1973.
24 Friedman, M. (with Rose), *Capitalism and Freedom*, University of Chicago Press, 1962.
25 Friedman, M. (with others), *Verdict on Rent Control*, IEA, 1972.
26 Friedman, M., *From Galbraith to Economic Freedom*, IEA, 1977.
27 Fulop, Christina, *Markets for Employment*, IEA, 1971.
28 Gray, H., *The Cost of Council Housing*, IEA, 1968.
29 Hailsham, Lord, *The Conservative Case*, Penguin, 1947, 1959.
30 Harris, R., in *Libraries: Free for All?*, IEA, 1962.
31 Harris, R. (with Seldon, A.), *Choice in Welfare*, 1963, 1965, 1970, IEA, 1971.
32 Harris, R. (with Seldon, A.), *Pricing or Taxing?*, IEA, 1976.
33 Hartwell, M., 'The Consequences for the Poor of the Industrial Revolution,' in *The Long Debate on Poverty*, IEA, 1972, 1974.
34 Hayek, F.A., *The Constitution of Liberty*, Routledge, 1960.
35 Hayek, F.A., *Full Employment at Any Price?*, IEA, 1975.
36 Hayek, F.A., *Choice in Currency*, IEA, 1976.
37 Hayek, F.A., *Denationalisation of Money*, IEA, 1976.
38 Hibbs, J., *Transport for Passengers*, IEA, 1963.
39 Hicks, J.R., *After the Boom*, IEA, 1966.
40 Hirschmann, A.O., *Exit, Voice and Loyalty*, Harvard, 1970.
41 Holland, J. and Perry, N., *Aspects of Leisure in Two Industrial Cities*, Social Science Research Council, 1976.
42 Houghton, Lord, *Paying for the Social Services*, IEA, 1967, 1968.
43 Howell, D., 'Instruments and Machinery for Control', in *Dilemmas of Government Expenditure*, IEA, 1976.
44 Huntford, R., *The New Totalitarians*, Allen Lane, 1975.
45 Hutt, W.H., *Politically Impossible?*, IEA, 1971.
46 Ireland, T.R., 'The Calculus of Philanthropy', in *The Economics of Charity*, IEA, 1973.
47 Jefferson, M., 'Industrialisation and Poverty: In Fact and Fiction', in *The Long Debate on Poverty*, IEA, 1972, 1974.
48 Jenkins, A., *The Case for Squash*, Jenkins, 1974.

49 Jenkins, A., 'Leisure Amenities and Local Authorities' (Ms), IEA, 1975.

50 Johnson, D.B., 'The Charity Market: Theory and Practice', in *The Economics of Charity*, IEA, 1973.

51 Johnson, H.G., *On Economics and Society*, University of Chicago Press, 1975.

52 Joseph, Sir K., *Reversing the Trend*, Barry Rose, 1975.

53 Keynes, J.M., *The End of Laissez Faire*, The Hogarth Press, 1926; *Collected Writings*, Macmillan, 1972.

54 Keynes, J.M., *The General Theory of Employment, Interest and Money*, Macmillan, 1936.

55 Keynes, J.M., 'The Balance of Payments of the United States,' *Economic Journal*, 1946.

56 Lange, O., 'The Computer and the Market', in Feinstein, C., *Capitalism, Socialism, and Economic Growth*, C.U.P., 1967.

57 Lees, D.S., *Health through Choice*, IEA, 1961.

58 Lenin, V.I., *State and Revolution* (1919).

59 Lindbeck, A., *The Political Economy of the New Left*, Harper & Row, 1971

60 Loughborough University, *The Swimming Pool Industry*, 1971.

61 Lynn, R., 'How Effective is Expenditure on Education?', in *The Dilemmas of Government Expenditure*, 1976.

62 McKenzie, R.B. and Tullock, G., *The New World of Economics*, Richard Irwin (USA), 1975.

63 Macrae, N., *To Let?*, IEA, 1960.

64 Marquand, D., 'A Social Democratic View', in *The Dilemmas of Government Expenditure*, IEA, 1976.

65 Maynard, A. (with King, D.), *Rates or Prices?*, IEA, 1972.

66 Maynard, A., *Experiment with Choice in Education*, IEA, 1975.

67 Meade, J.E., *The Just Economy*, Allen & Unwin, 1975.

68 Miller, M., *Rise of the Russian Consumer*, IEA, 1965.

69 Mishan, E.J., *The Costs of Economic Growth*, Pelican, 1967.

70 Nozick, R., *Anarchy, State and Utopia*, Basic Books (NY), 1974.

71 Olson, M., *The Logic of Collective Action*, Harvard, 1971.

72 Paine, T., *The Rights of Man* (1789), J.M. Dent.

73 Pardoe, J., 'Political Pressures and Democratic Institutions', in *The Dilemmas of Government Expenditure*, IEA, 1976.

74 Parker, R.A., 'Charging for Social Services', *Journal of Social Policy*, October 1976.

75 Peacock, A.T. (with Wiseman, J.), *Education for Democrats*, IEA, 1964.

76 Peacock, A.T. (with Shannon, R.), 'The Welfare State and the Redistribution of Income', in *Westminster Bank Review*, 1968.

77 Pennance, F.G. (with Gray, H.), *Choice in Housing*, IEA, 1968.

78 Pennance, F.G. (with West, W.A.), *Housing Market Analysis and Policy*, IEA, 1969.

79 Pennance, F.G., (Introduction), *Verdict on Rent Control*, IEA, 1972.

80 Peppiatt, W.D., 'Pricing of Seaside Facilities' in *The Theory and Practice of Pricing*, IEA, 1967.

81 Perlman, M., 'The Economics of Politics', in *The Vote Motive*, IEA, 1976.

82 Peston, M., *Public Goods and the Public Sector*, Macmillan, 1972.

83 Plant, Sir A., 'The Economic Theory concerning Patents for Inventions', *Economica*, 1934.

84 Plant, Sir A., 'The Economic Aspects of Copyright in Books', *Economica*, 1934.

85 Plant, Sir A., *The New Commerce in Ideas and Intellectual Property*, The Athlone Press, 1953.

86 Polanyi, G., *Comparative Returns from Investment in Nationalised Industries*, IEA, 1968.

87 Polanyi, G., *Contrasts in Nationalised Transport since 1947*, IEA, 1968.

88 Polanyi, G. (and others), *Policy for Poverty*, IEA, 1970.

89 Popper, Sir K., *The Open Society and its Enemies*, Routledge, 1966.

90 Prest, A.R., *Financing University Education*, IEA, 1966.

91 Robbins, Lord, *The Nature and Significance of Economic Science*, Macmillan, 1932.

92 Robbins, Lord, *The Theory of Economic Policy in English Classical Political Economy*, Macmillan, 1952.

93 Robbins, Lord, 'Notes on Public Finance', *Lloyds Bank Review*, 1955.

94 Robbins, Lord, *Political Economy Past and Present*, Macmillan, 1976.

95 Roth, G.J., *Paying for Parking*, IEA, 1965.

96 Roth, G.J., *A Self-Financing Road System*, IEA, 1966.

97 Rothbard, M.N., *Man, Economy and State*, Van Nostrand (USA), 1962.

98 Rothbard, M.N., *Power and Market*, Institute for Human Studies (USA), 1970.

99 Rothbard, M.N., *For a New Liberty*, Collier-Macmillan (NY), 1973.

100 Rowley, C.K. (with Peacock, A.T.), *Welfare Economics: A Liberal Restatement*, Martin Robertson, 1974.

101 Savas, E.S., 'Solid Waste Collection and Disposal', Graduate School of Business, of Columbia University, 1972.

102 Seldon, A., 'Which Way to Welfare', *Lloyds Bank Review*, 1965.

103 Seldon, A., *Taxation and Welfare*, IEA, 1967.

104 Seldon, A. (with Gray, H.), *Universal or Selective Social Benefits*, IEA, 1967.

105 Seldon, A., *After the NHS*, IEA, 1968.

106 Seldon, A., 'Taxing Social Benefits,' *Daily Telegraph*, 1968.

107 Seldon, A. (with Pennance, F.G.), *Everyman's Dictionary of Economics*, J.M. Dent, 1976.

108 Seldon, M., 'How Welfare Vouchers Work', *New Outlook*, June 1966.

109 Shenoy, Sudha, 'Pricing for Refuse Removal,' *The Theory and Practice of Pricing*, IEA, 1967.

110 Simey, M., *Municipal Review*, April, 1976.

111 Smith, A., *The Wealth of Nations* (1776), J.M. Dent.

112 Stigler, G.J., *The Citizen and the State*, Chicago University Press, 1975.

113 Tullock, G., *Private Wants, Public Means*, Basic Books (NY), 1970.

114 Tullock, G., *The Vote Motive*, IEA, 1976.

115 Vaizey, Lord, 'The Roulette of Public Spending', *New Statesman*, Feb. 1976.

116 West, E.G., *Education and the State*, IEA, 1965, 1970.

117 West, E.G., Education and the Industrial Revolution, Batsford, 1975.

118 West, E.G. (and others), *Regional Policy for Ever?*, IEA, 1973.

119 Wooldridge, W.C., *Uncle Sam, the Monopoly Man*, Arlington House (N.Y.) 1970.

Official Publications

121 *Economic Trends*, February 1976. 'Effects of Taxes and Benefits on Households,' Nissel, Muriel and Perez, Jane.

122 Layfield Report, Committee of Inquiry into Local Government Finance, 1976.

123 *Local Government Financial Statistics*, England & Wales, 1973-4, HMSO, 1975.

124 Plowden Report, *Children and their Primary Schools*, HMSO, 1967.

125 *Provision for Sport*, HMSO, 1972

126 *Road Pricing: The Economic and Technical Possibilities* (Smeed Committee), HMSO, 1964.

127 Sports Council, *Sport in the Seventies*, 1971.

Index

(Some numbers are the first of several pages in which the subject is discussed)